Table Of Contents

BIBLICAL ANSWERS FOR THE 21st CENTURY CHURCH

PAUL CANNINGS, D. Phil

Biblical Answers For The 21st Century Church
ISBN 0-9779840-3-6

Please send your comments and requests for information to the address below:

Power Walk Ministries
7350 West T.C. Jester Blvd.
Houston, TX 77088
Telephone: (281) 260-7402
www.lwfchurch.net/

Printed in the United States of America.

Scripture quotations are from the New American Standard Bible (NASB), unless otherwise noted.

For more information concerning other products we offer including:

"Making Your Vision A Reality" ISBN 0-9779840-2-8
"Keeping Love Alive Series" for strengthening marriages or the "Leadership Training Series" for training leaders,
visit our website at **www.lwfchurch.net/**

For more information about speaking engagements, please contact us by telephone at (281) 260-7402.

Introduction

Over the last 22 years of ministry, God has allowed me to be exposed to, and be a part of many difficult doctrinal issues that various churches encounter. During this time, I became involved in writing documents that served as a resource for many churches so that they can resolve issues from a "biblio-centric" perspective. The articles that are in this book are a compilation of the resources provided to these churches.

When Living Word Fellowship Church (the church I pastor) started, new papers were written and old papers were reviewed. This process created a lot of discussion among the leaders of the church. These men are trained men. Their biblical knowledge added to the strength of the papers presented in this book. Some of them were rewritten after being brought up for further discussion over the 11 years of the church's existence.

There are a number of times I have reviewed these papers so that I can add more biblical support for the various positions as God has exposed them to me. The constant analysis of these papers has led to many pastors, Bible teachers and church leaders requesting copies of them. Over the years, after God laid it on my heart to start Power Walk Ministries, several pastors who have used and found these papers to be extremely valuable to their church have asked if I would formulate these documents into a book. I have tried to make sure that each subject is exegetically addressed and that there are no denominational influences. I have approached the subjects based on word studies, grammar, historical and contextual reviews.

The focus is to make sure that the intent of the original author is prayerfully exposed, and the meaning of the text and its relation to the issue is exegetical defined. When Bible scholars are mentioned, it is because these men have shown great scholarship in addressing the various issues discussed in this book. Reference to these scholars is not based on a devotional commentary. It is based on their hermeneutical approach to the subject. Nevertheless, none of these scholars determined the final positions provided on each subject. They were used either to create contrast or to support what an exegetical study of the passage purported.

There is no desire on my part to make this study your decision on the issue. I strongly believe that each pastor or church leader must study the issue for themselves along with much prayer and a teachable spirit so that the Holy Spirit can guide them in and through the truth exposed in the Word of God. *"But you have an anointing from the Holy One, and you all know. I have not written to you because you do not know the truth, but because you do know it, and because no lie is of the truth"* (I John 2:20-22). These documents are a resource that a church may use to make decisions. This allows Christ's will to dominate the doctrine and structure of the church.

Christ's headship is functionally achieved when a church submits to the will of God and not the will of man. The will of man has historically influenced the church (whether this was the New Testament church or today's church) based on tradition or human philosophy. *"And he said to them, 'Rightly did Isaiah prophesy of you hypocrites, as it is written: 'this people honors me with their lips, but their heart is far away from me. But in vain do they worship me, teaching as doctrines the precepts of men. Neglecting the commandment of God, you hold to the tradition of men.' He was also saying to them, you are experts at setting aside the commandment of God in order to keep your tradition"* (Mark 7:6-10). *"Therefore as you have received Christ Jesus the Lord, so walk in him, having been firmly rooted and now being built up in him and established in your faith, just as you were instructed, and overflowing with gratitude. See to it that no one takes you captive through philosophy and empty deception, according to the tradition of men, according to the elementary principles of the world, rather than according to Christ"* (Colossians 2:6-9).

When the church is controlled by the power of God's Word, each leader or member has to submit their lives to Christ. Anytime a leader or member adjusts their life to Christ. The powerful transforming work of the Holy Spirit not only blesses the life of the church; he also blesses the life of the believer. This empowers each believer to live powerfully after collective worship is completed. This process leads to the Spirit of God functioning freely within the church (Ephesians 3:10; 14-19).

There are several of scripture references covered in this book. It is best for a pastor or leader to take time to read these references so the conclusions provided at the end of most chapters are clear. This can also provide an opportunity for leaders to discuss the various issues addressed in this book. Many churches that were served during the development of these papers were helped greatly because for the most part; it reduced the time it would have taken for a pastor or the leaders of the church to extensively research these topics.

It also created discussion that served to help many pastors understand how each of their leaders thought about the various issues that this book examines. This may lead to leaders eventually becoming of one mind, which serves to powerfully unite a congregation.

1

Believer's Baptism

The ordinances of baptism and communion are significant acts, which are at the center of the Church's expression of faith in the Lord Jesus Christ. It is important for believers in the Lord Jesus Christ to understand that baptism reflects the meaning of the Gospel because it involves both a relationship with Jesus Christ and fellow believers in the local church.

I. Why Baptize?

A. Baptism was commanded by the Lord Jesus Christ, "Go therefore and make disciples of all nations, baptizing them in the name of the Father and Son and the Holy Spirit" (Matthew 28:19). The Word of the Lord Jesus Christ is sufficient warrant for baptism of believers.

B. Baptism was practiced by the early Church. In the book of Acts, believers expressed publicly through the act of baptism, their inward decision and intention to submit to the Lord Jesus Christ as King (Acts 2; 41; 8:12-13; 36-38; 9:18; 10:44-48; 16:14-15; 32-33; 18:8; 19:5; 22:13-16).

II. Who Should Be Baptized?

A. Disciples - The Apostles were commanded to "make disciples of all the nations, baptizing them ... ." (Matthew 28:19). One must be a follower of Jesus Christ.

B. Believers - Individuals who personally trusted Jesus Christ as their own personal Savior. "Those who had received his word were baptized ... " (Acts 2:41). "But when they believed Philip preaching the good news about the kingdom of God and the name of Jesus Christ, they were being baptized, men and women alike" (Acts 8:12).

1. Anyone who has not been baptized since they became a Christian.

2. Any Christian who has never clearly understood the meaning of baptism even though they may have been baptized previously.

3. Any Christian who feels the need to renew their commitment to the Lord.

From the scriptures, we can conclude that baptism is limited to those who have personally trusted Jesus Christ as Savior and are willing to obey Him as Lord.

III. What Does Baptism Mean?

Definition: "Christian baptism is, in essence, the re-presentation of a man's renewal through his participation by means of the power of the Holy Spirit in the death and resurrection of Jesus Christ, and therewith the representation of man's association with Christ, with the covenant of grace which is concluded and realized in him, and with the fellowship of his Church" (The Teaching of Church Regarding Baptism, by Karl Barth).

A. The word "*baptido*" is "to dip or to plunge under water."

B. Baptism is a public declaration of the believer's identification with Jesus Christ in his death, burial, and resurrection. "Or do you not know that all of us who have been baptized into Christ Jesus have been baptized into his death? Therefore, we have been buried with him through baptism into death, in order that as Christ was raised from the dead through the glory of the Father, so we too might walk in newness of life" (Romans 6:3-4).

C. Baptism is a public declaration of the believer's identification with the Church. Baptism signifies the inward reality of a believer to participate in the fellowship of other believers in the context of a local church. The participation of the believer in baptism results in the believer being held accountable for his lifestyle and commitment by the local church.

D. Baptism is a symbolic proclamation of the spiritual reality of a believer's identification with Jesus Christ in his death, burial, and resurrection.

1. Death - Placed into the water; "Baptized into his death" (Romans 6:3).

2. Burial - Submerged; "Therefore, we have been buried with him through baptism into death...." (Romans 6:4a).

3. Resurrection - Brought up out of the water; "In order that as Christ was raised from the the dead through the glory of the Father, so we too might in newness of life" (Romans 6:4a; Colossians 3:1a).

E. So, we can see that baptism is important to the believer for the following reasons:

1. Baptism proclaims the believer's unity with Jesus Christ (Romans 6:1-10).

2. Baptism proclaims the believer's identification and accountability to the local church.

3. Baptism is a symbolic proclamation of the believer's saving experience with Jesus Christ.

4. Baptism proclaims the believer's commitment to be obedient to Jesus Christ.

5. Baptism is an expression of a repentant heart (Acts 2:38).

F. Baptism is a symbol not a mere sign for it actually illustrates the believer's death and resurrection with Christ.

G. Baptism is an act of faith and commitment. While faith is possible without baptism (i.e., salvation does not depend upon one's being baptized), baptism is a natural accompaniment and the completion of faith. So, baptism is a symbol of a believer's association with Christ and his suffering (Mark 10:38-39), the Gospel message, and with other believers.

IV. Is Salvation By Baptism?

We will review and analyze passages that will support salvation occurring as a result of baptism.

A. Mark 16:16: "He who believes and is baptized will be saved, but he who does not believe will be condemned." We must pay attention to the latter part of this verse. It is simply absence of belief not of baptism, which is correlated with condemnation.

B. John 3:5: "Unless one is born of water and the Spirit, he cannot enter the kingdom of God." What does born of water means to Nicodemus? It seems to favor the idea of cleansing or purification not baptism. Note that the emphasis throughout the passage is upon the Spirit and that there is no further reference to water.

C. I Peter 3:21: "Baptism, which corresponds to this, now saves you, not as a removal of dirt from the body but as an appeal to God for a clear conscience, through the resurrection of Jesus Christ." Note that this verse is actually a denial that the rite of baptism has any effect in itself. It saves only in that it is "an appeal to God," an act of faith acknowledging dependence, upon him. The real basis of our salvation is Christ's resurrection.

V. Repentance And Baptism

On the other side of the spectrum, there are some passages that tie repentance to baptism.

A. Acts 2:37-38 "Repent, and be baptized every one of you in the name of Jesus Christ of the forgiveness of your sins and you shall receive the gift of the Holy Spirit."

B. Acts 3:17-26: This passage emphasizes repentance as as necessary for conversion and acceptance of Christ and there is no mention of baptism.

C. Acts 16:31: And they said, "Believe in the Lord Jesus, and you shall be saved you and your household." **Note: There is no mention of baptism.**

D. Titus 3:5: "saved us, not because of deeds done by us in righteousness, but in virtue of his own mercy, by the washing of regeneration and renewal in the Holy Spirit."

Conclusion:

When all the implications are spelled out, this concept contradicts the principle of salvation by grace, which is so clearly taught in the New Testament. The insistence that baptism is necessary for salvation is something of a parallel to the insistenceof the Judaers that circumcision was necessary for salvation, a contention which Paul vigorously rejected in Galatians 5:1-12. Further, with the exception of the Great Commission, Jesus did not include the topic of baptism in his preching and teaching about the kingdom. Ideed, the thief on the cross was not, and could not have been baptized. Yet he was assured by Jesus, "Today you will be with me in Paradise."

Baptism is a testimony to the new life:

- New direction and purpose for living.
- Complete trust in God to direct your life.
- Courage and excitement to share Jesus Christ with others.
- Controlled and directed by the Holy Spirit (Galatians 5:16-24; Ephesians 4:17-6:20).
- Abandoning sinful habits and adopting godly habits (Colossians 3:1-4:6).

2

Discipline In The Local Church

I. The Definition:

Spiritual authority and accountability refers to the mutual and hierarchical responsibility of Christians to lovingly stimulate one another to faithful conformity to the rule of God in and through their lives so that he is glorified and his kingdom is promoted in the world (Dr. Anthony Evans). The general definition for accountability means to be answerable to someone, based on prescribed guidelines or responsibility.

II. Nature of Discipline:

The Church is a family of believers whose father is God. As in any family relationship, discipline for rebellious members of the family is a necessary requirement in order to develop character, as well as to maintain unity. Since God is the ideal father, he desires these same characteristics among his children. Therefore, he has commanded that the local church implement as part of its ministry, the loving discipline of rebellious members

(Hebrews 12:5-6, I Corinthians 5:1-13). The purpose of this is to reconcile these members back to God and the local body (I Corinthians 5:1-13; II Corinthians 2:6-8).The following is an example of the discipline process:

III. Biblical Overview Of Discipline:

A. General Overview:

1. Failure to obey God leads to universal sin and death (Genesis 1:16-17; 3:1-6; Romans 5:12; James 5:19 20).

2. Priests in Israel were killed for failing to worship God under proper authority (Leviticus 10:1-2).

3. God expects people to respect his ordained authorities and not resort to unbiblical means to accomplish biblical goals (I Samuel 24:2-22;19; 25; 26:9,11; 13:11-15).

4. God consigns physical death for rebellion against his authority in the Church (I Corinthians 5:5; 11:28-30; Acts 5:1-12).

B. The Spheres Of Biblical Authority And Accountability:

1. All members in the Trinity are equally God, yet, there is a line of authority (Philippians 2:5-11).

2. The Son willingly submitted himself to the authority of the Father (John 10:18; Luke 22:42; Hebrews. 5:2-9).

3. The Spirit submits himself to the authority of the Son (John 14:16-17; 16:5-15).

4. The Father holds the Son accountable for our sins (II Corinthians 5:21; Romans 3:25; 4:26; 8:3).

C. Authority And Accountability In The Church:

1. Believers are mutually responsible to one another (Philippians 2:3-4; Matthew 18).

2. Believers are to obey church leadership (Hebrews 13:17).

3. Deacons are accountable to the pastor (Acts 6:1-6; I Timothy 3:8-13) and the elders.

4. The pastor is accountable to God (Ephesians 4:11) and the elders (I Timothy 5:19-20).

5. The congregation is accountable for pastoral care (Galatians 6:6; Philippians 4:14-19; I Corinthians 9; I Timothy 5:17-18; I Thessalonians 5:12-13).

D. The Goal Of Biblical Authority And Accountability In The Church.

1. To establish and reflect the rule of God on earth through the church (Ephesians 1:18-23; 3:10).

2. To assure that church order is maintained (John 15:1-15; I Corinthians 5:6-7; I Timothy 3:15; Revelation 3:15-16).

3. To assure the effective execution of the ministry of the church through the use of spiritual gifts (Romans 12:3-8; Ephesians 4:11-16; I Corinthians 12; I Peter 4:10).

4. To promote a strong sense of family within the church (Ephesians 5:22-6:3).

5. To promote a context for responsible discipleship to occur (II Timothy 2;2; Titus 2:3-5).

E. The Need For Discipline

1. God is holy and demands the same from his children (Hebrews 12:11, I Peter 1:16).

2. Discipline impedes the spread of sin throughout the body so that the church can properly

function (I Corinthians 5:6-8).

3. Discipline purifies the church so that God is free to bless it as he desires (II Corinthians 7:10-12).

4. Discipline reveals the supernatural nature of the church (I Corinthians 6:1-11).

5. Discipline should be done with no partiality (I Timothy 5:21).

6. Discipline should not be done hastily, but with with deliberate steps (Matthew 18:15-20).

7. Discipline is correction focused on reconciliation. (II Corinthians 2:6-8).

8. The discipline of believers will allow God to have a greater influence upon unbelievers in our community and the world (I Peter 4:17; I Corinthians 5:12-13).

F. People That Should Be Disciplined:

1. An elder who is in sin (I Timothy 5:19-20).

2. Believers who are living unrepentant sinful lives (Matthew 18:15-17, I Corinthians 5:11-13).

3. Believers who are living undisciplined and irre-

sponsible lives (II Thessalonians 3:6-15).

4. Believers who are causing divisiveness within the church (Romans 16:17-18; Titus 2:9-10; 3:8-11; I Timothy 6:3-5; II Timothy 2:14-19; II Timothy 2:23-26; James 5:9; Colossians 3:13).

5. Believers who are living immoral lives (I Corinthians 5:1-5).

6. Believers who are promoting false doctrine in in the church (I Timothy 1:18-20; Titus 1:10-16; II Peter 2; Ezekiel 34; Hosea 4:6).

7. A brother who has been overtaken by sin (Galatians 6:1).

G. The Objectives Of Discipline:

1. To warn others of the serious consequences of sin (Acts 5:1-11; I Timothy 5:20).

2. To encourage repentance and restoration of the sinning believer to the church (I Timothy 1:20; II Corinthians 2:6-7; 7:10- 22).

3. To prevent the church from further decay and challenge members to godliness (I Corinthians 5:7-8; Galatians 6:1; I Timothy 5:20).

4. To secure the eternal salvation of the sinning be-

liever even though it may mean physical death (I Corinthians 5:5; 11:27-34; James 5:19-20).

5. To demonstrate God's love for his children (Hebrews 12:6).

6. To remove the defilement and leavening influence that sin brings (I Corinthians 5:6-8).

7. To produce soundness in faith (Titus 1:13).

H. The Attitude Of Discipline:

1. Discipline is to be exercised in an attitude of humility, recognizing that one day the tables could be turned (Galatians 6:1).

2. Discipline is to be exercised in an attitude of prayer (Matthew 18:19-20).

3. Discipline is to be exercised in an attitude of forgiveness if the sinning believer repents (II Corinthians 2:7; 2:5-11; 7:10-13).

4. Discipline is to be exercised in an attitude of of love (II Corinthians 2:4).

5. Uncompromising stand against sin (Titus 1:13).

I. The Procedures Of Discipline:

1. First, a private appeal for repentance is to be made to the sinning brother.

2. Secondly, if the believer does not repent in the private meeting, an additional person(s) is/are to go in and attempt to encourage repentance as well as to witness the facts involved.

3. Thirdly, if there is still no openness to repentance, the brother and his sin is to be brought before the whole church and the church is to appeal to him to repent.

4. If the believer does not repent or show a willingness to submit to the leadership of the church, the believer's name will be removed from the church's membership roll. The believer will then lose all of the rights and privileges of membership.

    a. **Note:** During this state, the sinning believer is still viewed as a brother and is to be counseled, encouraged, and admonished.

    b. If the believer repents and submits to spiritual leadership at any stage of the disciplinary process, the believer is then restored to full fellowship with the church.

IV. Discipline And Restoration (Matthew 18:15-20; I Corinthians 5; II Corinthians 2:1-11):

A. Discipline:

1. The discipline process should start with an individual exhortation to repentance from believer to believer.

2. If the sinning believer does not repent, the discipline process should continue with two or three people encouraging repentance and establishing the facts. This group should also include a leader who is closest to the situation (i.e., care cell leader, ministry head, deacon, elder or pastoral staff).

3. If rebellion (refusal to deal with the prescribed action necessary to deal with their sin) continues, the identification of the sinning believer is to be brought before the elders. In addition, a certified letter is to be sent to the person in question informing them that unless they begin dealing with their sin, they will be publicly brought before the congregation (this should be done within one month of the letter). If they are prepared to deal with their sin, then they are to respond to an assigned elder. Such sincere efforts will cancel the public announcement of their rebellion. During this time the person must be re-

moved from all ministry responsibility.

4. If there is no positive response to the letter, the discipline process continues by bringing the believer (or his name) before the whole congregation (probably best around communion). The congregation is encouraged to pray for, and admonish the errant member. During this time in addition to not participating in ministry, there is to be a withdrawal of fellowship so that the person cannot enjoy full partcipation in the life, activities, and benefits of the church. The one exception to this is the general corporate worship of the church (except communion).

5. If there is still no repentance over the next 30 days, another certified letter is to be sent informing the rebellious member that they will be excommunicated from the church on the date designated (within 30 days). It is to be communicated that this action can be stopped if they will deal with their rebellion and that the church stands ready and willing to assist them.

6. Finally, if there is still no response, there is to be a total withdrawal of fellowship by excommunicating the sinning believer from the church.

Note: As long as a sinning believer shows signs of attempting to deal with their sin, efforts should be made to assist and encourage them. We must error on the side of grace. It should be a general goal to accomplish the full discipline process within a six-month period from the time it reaches the elders.

B. Discipline Process For One Who Attends Church Inconsistently:

1. If we confront a sinning brother or sister about a sin issue and they are attending church regularly, we will continue the disciplinary process even if the person stops attending regularly.

2. If we find that a person has been sinning during a two-month period of time (this is because if a person is missing for two months, we automatically remove them from the church role) and that person has not attended church, we will not confront that person about their sin.

3. If at any time during any of the above situations, the person requests either verbally or by written letter to end their membership at Living Word Fellowship Church, the disciplinary process will stop.

C. Restoration:

1. When repentance is made, restoration should be given to the sinning brother on the same level in which the discipline was applied.

2. There should be an appropriately assigned leader and/or fellow believer assigned to the repentant believer to help them deal with any adjustments that need to be made as they seek to reestablish themselves in the body.

3. They are to become active again in the ministry and benefits of the church in accordance to what is deemed appropriate to each individual case with counseling continuing as needed.

Note: When children who are members and are living at home with believing parents are involved in the discipline or restoration process, the parents should be involved as much as possible in the process.

3

Choreographed Dancing During Worship

Introduction

There is no question that dancing did occur on many occasions during worship. Worshippers in their excitement and joy would spontaneously worship God in song and dance. There is no command that instructs believers to dance during worship and there is no pattern that the New Testament Church danced during worship. When the Church first began in Acts 2:42-47, members did not dance, nor were they instructed to dance. The focus of the service seems to be more concentrated around the Lord's Supper, the teaching of the Word, prayer and fellowship. In the New Testament, the churches in Ephesus were told to raise their hands in worship (I Timothy 2:8).

Most of the dancing that took place in worship occurred in the Old Testament. Worshippers, especially women, would many times be encouraged to dance. This chapter will address this issue by reviewing dancing in the various forms of dancing, dancing as a spontaneous reaction to the wondrous works of God, and the purpose of dancing as portrayed in the Word.

I. The Various Reasons Worshippers Danced

A. They danced to celebrate the wonderful works of God (Exodus 15:22; Jeremiah 31:4-6).

B. Dancing took place as the people praised the Lord (Psalm 149:1-4; 150:1-6).

C. Dancing occurred when the Israelites experienced times of victory (I Samuel 18:6; Judges 11:34).

D. When God reestablishes His kingdom the people of Israel will dance (Jeremiah 31:12-16).

II. Dancing That Was Not An Act Of Worship

A. When the prodigal son returned home, his father had a feast that included dancing (Luke 15:22-25).

B. The sons of Benjamin took for themselves wives while the women were dancing (Judges 21:19-24).

C. Herod had a birthday party and it is at this party that the daughter of Herodias asks for the head of John the Baptist (Mark 6:21-23).

D. Sinners danced at the sound of the flute and had no desire for God (John 21:11-14).

E. The children of Israel danced and worshipped the

calf while Moses worshipped God on Mount Sinai (Exodus 32:19).

F. Jesus compared the children of Israel to those who dance at a wedding and with those who dance at a funeral (Matthew 11:16-18).

G. Solomon said; "A time to weep, and a time to laugh; a time to mourn, and a time to dance." (Ecclesiastes 3:4).

III. Dancing as a Spontaneous Response to God

A. As David returned from killing the Philistines, the women of all the cities of Israel came out dancing (I Samuel 18:6).

B. When David dedicated the building materials of the temple and felt revived in his spirit, he danced (Psalm 30:11-12).

C. Most times this would occur with women who danced spontaneously before God (Exodus 15:20-21; Judges 21:19-21; 1 Samuel 18:6). **Note:** There are two exceptions to this and they are found in Jeremiah 31:13 and Job 21:11.

IV. A Biblical Overview of Dancing

A. Dancing served as an emotional response to the wondrous acts of God. It was a response to how God responded to his people either during times of war or times of restoration.

B. It seemed to be an expression of praise to God.

C. In most of the references in the Bible when there was dancing during worship, women were doing the dancing. There are only two occasions when men danced in worship (Jeremiah 31:13; II Samuel 6:14).

D. Dancing was not limited to worship. People danced to celebrate birthdays etc.

E. Dancing on every occasion was spontaneous it was never a choreographed performance in worship.

F. The Bible does not speak out against dancing within the context of the passages mentioned in this chapter.

G. There is no record that when the churches in the New Testament gathered for worship – they danced. There was more attention placed on the Lord's Supper (Acts 2:42-44; 20:7), singing (Colossians 3:15-17), prayer (Acts 2:42; I Timothy 2:8), teaching (Acts 2:42) and fellowship (Acts 2:42; Hebrews 10:24-26).

H. When Paul instructs Timothy as a pastor concerning worship in I Timothy 2, he never mentions choreographed dancers.

4

Divorce and Remarriage

Introduction

Divorce was permitted in the Old Testament (Deuteronomy 24:1-4; Malachi 2:13-17) as well as in the New Testament (Matthew 5:31-32; 19:1-12; I Corinthians 7:12-16; Romans 7:1-4). God in the Old Testament said he hated it (Malachi 2:16), and Christ in the New Testament says, "... that what God put together, let no man separate." (Matthew 19:6). It is obvious when man vowed before witnesses to be married until death, God solidified this covenant in heaven (Romans 7:1-4). God from this point forward will determine how the marriage functions (I Corinthians 11:3; Ephesians 5:21-33), and how it can end.

Marriage is not man's idea. It is God's plan for mankind. When two individuals enter into holy matrimony, they must understand that their commitment is to God and then to each other. This study will first examine divorce, and then we will outline biblically who can remarry, and how this all works itself out at Living Word Fellowship Church.

I. The Meaning And Significance Of The Marriage Covenant

A. A covenant is not the same as a contract. A contract is an agreement that two parties have mutually agreed to fulfill. A covenant, on the other hand, is a process that we enter into where someone (God) serves as the overseer, and he governs the conditions of the covenant (Malachi 2:14).

B. God does not break covenants (Leviticus 26:42).

C. God calls the marriage a covenant in Malachi 2:14 and Proverbs 2:17. He says that he serves as a witness between the man and his wife (Genesis 31:50).

D. When a man and woman make their wedding vows, they begin the process of establishing the marriage covenant before God (Numbers 30; Psalm 116:14, 18).

The meaning of the word "vow":

A vow is a solemn promise or pledge that binds a person to perform a specified act or to behave in a certain manner. The first mention of a vow in the Bible is of Jacob at Bethel (Genesis 28:20-22; 31:13). Other people who made a vow are Jephthah (Judges 11:30-31,39), Hannah (I Samuel 1:11), David (Psalm 132:2-5), and Absalom (II Samuel 15:7-8). All vows were made to God as a promise in expectation of his favor (Genesis 28:20) or in thanksgiving for his blessings (Psalm 116:12-14). Vowing might be a part of everyday devotion (Psalm 61:8) or the annual festivals (I Samuel 1:21). Vows must be paid to God in the congregation at the tabernacle or temple (Deuteronomy 12:6,11; Psalm 22:25). (Nelson's Illustrated Bible Dictionary Copyright (C) 1986, Thomas Nelson Publishers).

E. Sexual intimacy solidifies the marriage covenant. (Genesis 2:24).

God says in Genesis that a husband and wife are one flesh. Paul teaches what this means in I Corinthians 6:16 where he repeats what God said in Genesis 2:24. *"Or do you not know that the one who joins himself to a harlot is one body with her?* For Paul says, "The two will become one flesh." Christ said this, when talking about divorce in Matthew 19:4-6.

Like the Apostle Paul, Christ, in Matthew 19:4-6, supports His point, in this passage, by repeating Genesis 2:24. This is why the writer of Hebrews said, *"Let marriage be held in honor among all, and let the marriage bed be undefiled; for fornicators and adulterers God will judge"* (Hebrews 13:4). Sexual intimacy solidifies the marriage covenant. This is why when a husband and wife are sexually intimate on the wedding night, and if the wife is a virgin the woman expels blood. All covenants are solidified with blood (Genesis 15:4-18; John 19:17-22).

In summary, God is the overseer and governor of the marriage and the marriage covenant. Everyone who enters into marriage is accountable to him. He sets the conditions for the marriage and the resolution of the marriage.

II. Marriage Is Permanent And Must Never Be Broken

A. Definition for this view:

The definition of this view is that the exception Christ addressed in Matthew 19:9 was not for adultery in the manner in which we interpret the word. It was related to Herod Antipas marrying his brother's ex-wife which violated Leviticus 18:6-20, because he had an incestuous relationship with her. This marriage was unlawful as John the Baptist stated (Matthew 14:4) because of what was outlined by Moses in Leviticus 18:6-20. As a result Christ was not supporting the Shammai or Hellel view. Christ was supporting the original view (Matthew 19:4-6); *"Consequently they are no longer two, but one flesh. What therefore God has joined together let no man separate."*

B. Historical background to Matthew 19 that supports this position:

In Leviticus 18:6-20 God, through Moses speaks out against all forms of relationships that displeases him. (Paul uses this to speak out against the man in I Corinthians 5:1-8). This is why John the Baptist speaks out (Leviticus 18:16; 20:21) against Herod Antipas in Matthew 14. However, Herod's wife encourages her daughter to talk Herod into having John the Baptist beheaded for speaking out against their marriage.

As a result John the Baptist is beheaded and his head head is brought to Herod on a platter. Jesus was passing through territory that was under the jurisdiction of Herod Antipas. The Pharisees were trying to trap Jesus because they knew that Jesus held to the same beliefs as John the Baptist. If Jesus had repeated what John the Baptist said then maybe they could have him killed as well. Jesus, however, avoided confrontation with Herod Antipas by stating that because Herod's sexual intimacy with his brother's wife was incestuous, since this violated Leviticus 18:6-18 the divorce was legal.

They viewed the uncovering of his brother's wife's nakedness as incestuous. So Jesus did not say that Herod's marriage was unlawful, because this could have cost him his life. Since Herod Antipas was now intimate with his brother's wife uncovering her nakedness and developing incestuous relations (in violation of Leviticus 18:16; 20:21), the divorce of his wife from his brother was now biblically correct. Christ did not say that they were committing adultery as John the Baptist had said. This was not Christ's appointed time to die, so he avoided confrontation with Herod Antipas.

"Jesus followed John in condemning incestuous marriage, but while John declared directly, "It is not lawful," Jesus avoided a confrontation with Herod Antipas by simply stating that in the case of such an unlawful marriage, divorce was permitted." (Quote from page 76 of The Divorce Myth by J. Carl Laney.) Therefore their argument is divorce could not occur for any reason, and it was only because Herod Antipas slept with his brother's wife, creating incestuous relations, that he violated Leviticus 18:16; 20:21 and sinned.

C. Refutation:

Nowhere in Matthew 14:1-12 is it indicated that this was

an incestuous relationship or that John the Baptist or Christ in Matthew 19 viewed it as incestuous. The Webster Dictionary defines incest as "sexual intercourse between persons too closely related to marry legally." J. Carl Laney has interpreted this relationship as illegal because it violates Leviticus 18. This is why he states that it is incestuous. But I do not think that an exegetical interpretation of Leviticus 18 would support that uncovering someone's brother's wife's nakedness is incestuous. It was just wrong.

Christ in Matthew 19:9 said "whoever divorces his wife, ... and marries another woman (any woman)." It seems as if Christ is speaking generally, not to specific family members or to someone's brother's wife. The key issue for Christ since sexual intimacy binds people together as one (Matthew 19:5) is the breaking of the bond as a result of (Matthew 19:9) immorality. Breaking the bond of marriage is quite clear when we read I Corinthians 6:16 *"Or do you not know that the one who joins himself to a harlot is one body with her?* For he says, "The two will become one flesh." The issue for Christ does not seem to be incest, but the violation of a covenant. Hebrews 13:4 states *"Let marriage be held in honor among all, and let the marriage bed be undefiled; for fornicators and adulterers God will judge."*

D. Concluding remarks for this section:

Jesus is not talking about an incestuous relationship but is addressing the "indecency" that Moses addresses in Deuteronomy. This would have better served to answer the question of the Pharisees and Scribes. This passage does not support the view outlined above; rather it supports those who believe that adultery is the essential provision for divorce.

III. The Problem Of Matthew 19 With Mark 10:4-12 If The Exception For Divorce Is Adultery:

Even though Mark was speaking to a different audience (the Romans) than Matthew (the Jews), Mark (Mark 10:4-12) did not give any exceptions for divorce. Mark seems to view marriage as permanent and if anyone divorces their mate and remarries, they commit adultery. If Matthew 19 provides an exception in the case of adultery, then this view contradicts what Mark is saying in verses 11-12 of chapter 10. Mark does not allow divorce for any exception. Mark 10:11-12 states – *"And he saith unto them, Whosoever shall put away his wife, and marry another, committeth adultery against her. And if a woman shall put away her husband, and be married to another, she committeth adultery."*

Refutation:

The book of Mark is a short abbreviation of the Gospels. I tend not to view Matthew 19 and Mark 10:4-12 as a contradiction but like anything else in the Bible one Book fills in for us what another Book did not include. This is what makes all the books in the Bible important for each other and allows the Bible, as a whole, to be complete. Therefore, this is not a contradiction because Mark is not saying that the divorced couple will commit adultery even if the reason they divorced was adultery. Mark does not say if they divorce, for any reason, they commit adultery when they remarry.

Mark would not say this, I believe, because Mark knows what Moses says in Deuteronomy 24:1-4. Mark addresses this issue generally; whereas, Matthew addresses it more specifically.

IV. Christ's Use Of The Greek Supports Marriage Being Permanent:

There are two major Greek words that are used for unlawful sexual behavior. *Moicheia* is used primarily for adultery, which means sexual unfaithfulness to a marriage covenant. *Porneia* from which we get the word *porne*, which means, "to sell," was related to "a harlot for hire." So this word came to be related to prostitution or fornication. It was also used for homosexuality (Romans 1:29) and incest (I Corinthians 5:1). It can also mean adultery, but this is not its normal usage. So *porneia* is a more general term for unlawful sexual relations (I Corinthians 6:13; II Corinthians 12:21; Galatians 5:19).

The term that Jesus used in Matthew 19:9 is *porneia*. The supporters of this view will ask the question; "If Jesus was speaking of adultery, why didn't he use *moichea* rather than *porneia*?" They provide five possible solutions to this problem. The one that the supporters of this view held to the most (supported by noted scholars such as F.F. Bruce and Charles C. Ryrie) was the interrelation of this passage to Leviticus 18:6-18.

Therefore, Jesus was teaching that if a person was to commit incest, or marry his brother's wife or do what the man in I Corinthians 5:1-8 did then divorce would be permitted. Divorce was not permitted under any other circumstances. Therefore, Jesus was not agreeing with the Shammai view (when Moses said indecent in Deuteronomy 24:1, he meant adultery) or the Hellel view (when Moses said indecent he meant anything. They emphasize the part of the verse that says, "she finds no favor in his eyes," but they leave out "because he has found some indecency with her."). This is why, supporters of this view claim that Jesus disciples said, *"If the relationship of the man with his wife is like this, it is better not to marry."* Also, the Pharisees who supported the Shammai or the Hellel view, were silent after Jesus provided his explanation, showing that they understood that he did not support either views and they could not trap him.

If Jesus explained what this view believes, they would have trapped him. They believed that Jesus was teaching that a man and woman were bound together for life. "*. . . What God has joined together, let no man separate" (Matthew 19:6).* This, the supporters of this view say, then supports Mark 10:4-12 and Luke 16:18 i.e., if anyone divorces and then remarries they commit adultery. (Mark uses the specific Greek word for adultery, *moichea*). Also, it lines up with Paul in Romans 7:1-4; *"For the married woman is bound by law to her husband while he is living; but if her husband dies, she is released from the law concerning the husband."* Paul says the same thing in I Corinthians 7:39; *"A wife is bound as long as her husband lives; but if her husband is dead, she is free to be remarried to whom she wishes, only in the Lord."*

Refutation:

The *porneia*, which means "unlawful sexual relations," does not eliminate Christ from allowing adultery as an exception. This was an unlawful relationship between Herod Antipas and Herodias. It violated Leviticus 18:16 and 20:21, and I am sure that when Moses wrote Deuteronomy 24:1-4 he was not speaking in violation of Leviticus 18:16 or 20:21. Yet, he allowed divorce for "some indecency." Matthew 14:1-12 does not describe Herod Antipas as sexually unfaithful to his wife before marrying Herodias. This would be marital unfaithfulness *moicheia.* It describes him as divorcing his wife and marrying his brother's wife.

So Herod Antipas was not sexually unfaithful while married to his wife. However, the relationship he was involved in was unlawful because he uncovered the nakedness of his brother's wife in violation of Leviticus 18:16 or 20:21. Therefore, it is more appropriate for Christ to use *porneia* then *moicheia.*

IV. The Biblical Meaning And Conditions For Divorce

Note: Some of the information in this section is taken from Dr. Anthony Evans' position paper on this subject.

A. We must first bear in mind the following biblical principles:

1. God meant for there to be one man and one woman for life (Matthew 19:6-8; Romans 7:1 4).

2. God directly states that he hates divorce Malachi 2:16).

3. God pronounces punishment on those who get divorced (Malachi 2:10,16).

4. Christ states in Matthew 19:6; "Consequently, they are no longer two, but one flesh. What therefore God has joined together let no man separate."

5. Even though Christ permits divorce for reasons we will outline below, he still would rather us

forgive rather than divorce. The book of Hosea illustrates this concept for us.

B. Definition Of Divorce:

It is a legal dissolution of a marriage relation, a decree dissolving a marriage. From a Biblical perspective, the elders of the church cannot allow this decree, unless the divorce fits within God's guidelines.

C. God Permits Divorce:

1. God allowed Moses to write a bill of divorce (Deuteronomy 24:1-4).

2. Jesus says in Matthew 19:9 that if one of the partners commits adultery then the other person can file for divorce.

3. Paul states that if an unbeliever deserts a believer and divorces the believer, then the believer is free from the marriage (I Corinthians 7:15). **Note:** This may have had ties to the Old Testament. In Ezra 9-10 (Malachi 2:11; Nehemiah 13: 23-31) the Jews were ordered to divorce their Gentile wives because it was unlawful for a Jew to marry a Gentile. This was to preserve the Jewish nation from becoming polluted with foreign blood and religions. In the New Testament, the unbeliever (Gentile) must be the one who desires to leave (I Corinthians 7:12-13). The unbe-

liever cannot be sent away.

4. If one of the partners dies, the other is free from the marriage (Romans 7:1-4).

5. The only reason that Christ states that divorce occurs is the hardness of people's heart (Matthew 19:8).

D. God limits the reasons for getting a divorce:

1. People cannot get a divorce for just any reason (Matthew 19:13-16).

2. Adultery (immorality) is the only grounds given by Christ as an acceptable reason for divorce (Matthew 19:9).

3. Abandonment of a believer by an unbeliever (I Corinthians 7:15).

4. Forgiveness and reconciliation takes precedence over even legitimate grounds for divorce (Matthew 5:23-26).

Summary:

1. God hates divorce because marriage is a covenant that he has established and he expects us because of our respect for him, to uphold it.

2. Marriage highlights Christ and the Church. For a man and woman to divorce is to put an end to something that Christ will complete when he presents us before God. It also removes the ill-ustration of how Christ functions relevant to the Church before the world. This is why a man must first have his home in order before he is allowed ed to lead in the church.

3. The Word of God is objective, and it is perfect. When couples divorce for irreconcilable differ-ences, it is because one or both individuals refuse to submit to the Word.

4. Divorce should be discouraged at all cost since it is not God's ideal way.

Remarriage after Divorce

1. Remarriage was allowed for divorced individ-uals in the Old Testament (Deuteronomy 24:1-4). Christ in Matthew 19:9 informs us that the reason, why Moses was allowing divorce was adultery, because this violated the marriage covenant as described above.

2. Jesus recognized that divorced people would be placed in the posture of remarriage and would have a desire to remarry (Matthew 5:31-32). It is not his ideal, but he reconizes that the need will

arise. In the same way God acknowledges that this need will arise in Deuteronomy 24:1-4.

3. Even though God hates divorce, he allowed marriage relationships outside of his ideal (David and Bethseba, Jacob, and Solomon). Christ did the same thing with the Samaritan woman in John 4.

4. If a person wishes to remarry and they were divorced for unbiblical reasons, they can remarry recognizing that they would need to confess their sin before God and repent. When they have genuinely completed this, they can then remarry with a commitment to sin no more (the Samaritan woman in John 4:15-19).

5. Remarriage can occur without sin when the reasons for divorce fit within biblical guidelines as outlined in this chapter.

6. Remarriage is not God's ideal way, but to remarry is not an unforgivable sin.

5

Eternal Security

The Problem:

Many people argue that if a person, who believes in Christ and in his death and resurrection, but does not consistently live a Christian life they will eventually lose their eternal life and will once again be doomed for hell. They believe that a person does not gain their salvation by works, but they maintain their salvation by their consistent obedience to God's Word.

I. Why People Lack Assurance Of Their Salvation

A. Some people forget the time when they actually were saved. However, they may probably remember getting baptized but not saved.

B. Some people are not sure that they are saved because they were not sure they did everything correctly. They remain unsure for the following reasons:

1. They are not sure that they said the right words when they prayed.

2. They did not feel anything.

3. They knew what they did, but they were somewhat intoxicated when they accepted Christ as their Savior.

4. They have seen many people accept Christ only to live a contradictory life style a few days, weeks or years later.

5. Because of some controversial passages such as:

   a) Hebrews 6:1-8;
   b) John 15:1-17;
   c) 1 John 4:4-10;
   d) 1 Corinthians 9:24-27.

II. Passages That Assure Believers Of Their Salvation:

A. God never promises to give believers life that is temperate or conditional, but *eternal life* (John 3:16,18,36; 5:24; 6:47; I John 2:25; Titus 1:2) that is a gift (Romans 6:23). This life is provided not because of our works but because of his grace (Ephesians 2:8-9).

B. After John has explained, in John 10:1-21 that Jesus is the "Good Shepherd" who laid down his life for his sheep and picked it up again and that the "Good

Shepherd" is also the Gate, John then states in verses 28-29 that "*and I give eternal life to them, and they shall never perish; and no one shall snatch them out of my hand. My Father, who has given them to me, is greater than all; and no one is able to snatch them out of the Father's hand.*" Please notice that he mentions twice "<u>no one</u> is able to snatch them."

C. The Bible also states that we are not holding on to God, he is the one who is protecting us (I Peter 1:3-6; Jude 24-25; John 10:28).

D. Christ also promises that all who believe in Him shall be raised up in the last day, and He will not lose anyone (John 6:39-40).

E. If "*greater is he who is in you than he who is in the world,*" (I John 4:4) then how can Satan steal us from Christ, especially when "*in all things we overwhelmingly conquers through him who loved us*" (Romans 8:37). Please remember that the Word of God also states that "*nor any other created things, <u>shall be able to separate us from the love of God</u>, which is in Christ Jesus our Lord*" (Romans 8:39).

F. We are hidden in Christ (Colossians 3:3), and cannot be separated from his love (Romans8:39). How can we lose our salvation?

G. Children who are born into a family cannot be unborn (John 3:1-15).

H. When believers sin, Christ says, "He is faithful and righteous to forgive us our sins and to cleanse us from all unrighteousness," not dump us out of heaven.

I. Since I am saved by grace and not of myself, then how can I lose it as a result of myself? How can I lose life that was given by grace? The fact that I was saved by grace is proof that God knew that I would still make mistakes as a believer (this is why God told Paul His grace was sufficient), so he provided grace not so that I would sin more, but so that his grace, which is proof of His love, would cause me to mature.

III. Summary Response To Controversial Passages Listed Above:

A. Hebrews 6:1-8: This passage is speaking to believers who like the Israelites in the wilderness had experienced God but decided to do whatever they wanted to do. As a result, instead of experiencing the promised land they were judged. In other words, believers who who turn away, and continue to live ungodly lives, will be judged (just like the Israelites, therefore will be unable to return to Christ, in the manner in which they were).

B. John 15:1-17: The issue here is not losing our salvation, but rather who are Christ's disciples (15:8, if someone wants to experience God's abiding power he must obey God's Word).

C. I John 4:4-10: The issue here is that Gnostic philosophers state that believers can continue to live the way they used to live because Christ lived on the inside not outside. So, John was making a distinction between those who say they are saved and those who are not. The issue was not gaining or losing salvation.

D. I Corinthians 9:24-27: Paul, in this passage, is discussing winning rewards, not losing salvation.

Conclusion:

It is impossible to lose salvation when we do not earn it, or gain what you do not have the power to provide.

6

A Biblical Description Of Healing Found In James 5:14-15

Introduction

It is necessary to discuss this subject in view of all that has been said and done in many churches, and on television. Therefore the purpose of this chapter is to provide a biblical outline relevant to this subject.

I. Biblical Evaulation of Healing as it Relates to God, Christ and the Apostles

A. Healing and Christ's atonement based on Isaiah 53:4 and Matthew 8:17:

Many people believe based on Isaiah 53:4-5 and Matthew 8:17 that as a result of Christ's death not only was salvation provided, but we were also healed from physical illnesses. Those who perpetuate this view, believe that illnesses have come into existence as a result of Adam's sin, mankind's fall from God's presence. Therefore sin has a spiritual origin, and can only be removed as a result of Christ's death, God's atonement for mankind's sins. Therefore, the potential for healing of the body took place when Christ died, so that all who have faith in Christ, for salvation and healing can be released from spiritual and physical illnesses.

However, Jesus did not make this connection in John 9:2-3. The disciples raised the question, "Who sinned, this man or his parents?" Jesus replied, "It was neither that this man sinned, nor his parents; but it was in order that the works of God might be displayed in him." Jesus did not link the sins of man to the unforgiveness of sin, nor did he tie the healing of the blind man to the forgiveness of sin. It is obvious that the Pharisees believed like the disciples did (John 9:13-34). Also, Jesus came back and approached the man, talking to him about believing in the "Son of Man" at which point the man worshipped him (vs. 38), demonstrating two completely separate developments. Jesus healed him because this glorified God then Jesus approached him to deal with his sinfulness.

It was also clear that healing had more to do with faith than with the forgiveness of sins. Either the person who was healed needed faith, or the bearer of the person who needed to be healed needed faith. The New Testament provides us with many examples, such as the woman with an issue of blood for 12 years (Matthew 9:20-22), the ten lepers (Luke 17:11-19), Bartimaeus, the blind beggar (Mark 10:46-52), the Syrophoenician woman's daughter (Mark 7:24-30), the centurion's servant (Matthew 8:5-13), and the demoniac boy (Mark 9:14-29). There is no mention of forgiveness of sins in any of these instances, just the need for faith. What Isaiah and Matthew are saying is that Jesus incarnate "bore" or "carried" in his human flesh, all the sickness, sorrow, and physical infirmities that we may experience, so that he can "sympathise with our very weakness" (Hebrews 4:15). This also allowed Christ to be fully human, therefore becoming a perfect sacrifice for mankind (Romans 12:12-21). The only thing that Christ made atonement for was our sins not our physical weakness. What point would it be for Christ to die to give us perfect bodies when it is our spirit that goes to heaven when we die, and we will all have glorified bodies at the resurrection (I Corinthians 15:42-44)?

In Isaiah 53:5, the subject is Christ removing our transgression not our physical ailments. Matthew 8:17 also describes healing that occurred sometime before Christ's death. Therefore, Matthew's quote of Isaiah could not justify these individuals belief that Christ's death removed our disease.

B. Summary of healing as it relates to God and Christ:

1. A General Overview:

First, we must establish that God has always been viewed as the healer. In Psalm 103:3, the psalmist says "Who [God] pardons all your iniquities; who heals all your diseases." God is also viewed as the one who can give sickness and disease because of Israel's disobedience (Deuteronomy 28; 32:39; Numbers 12:9-15; II Chronicles 21:18-19; 26:16-21). Even though medical practice was used in the Old Testament, (II Kings 20:7; II Kings 16:12;) in the New Testament Jesus did not see anything wrong with people consulting a physician (Matthew 9:12) healing was always attributed to God (Exodus 4:24-26; II Kings

1; 20: 1-11; I Kings 13:4-6; 17:17-24; Numbers 21:6-9). In Exodus 15:26, God declares himself to Moses as Jehovah-Rophi, "I, the Lord, am your healer."

God also disciplines his children through sickness (Proverbs 3:7-8, 11-12), and will develop faith, humility, and character as a result of sickness (Job 40:4; 42:6). This also occurs in the New Testament for all believers (Hebrews 12:6; John 5:14), and for Paul (II Corinthians 4:17). In the Old Testament, believers viewed healing of sickness as the supernatural intervention of God. Sickness was an evil that God might allow man to experience because man insisted on violating his law. In the New Testament, faith in Christ's healing ministry was extremely important. It seems to be mostly attached to the faith of the person being healed or the person who is requesting the healing. Faith was a prerequisite for healing, and was present before Christ responded to the need of the individual to be healed (Matthew 9:2,22,29; 8:13; 15:28).

The powerful transformation that occurred at Jesus' command was most of the times attributed to the faith of the individual requesting the healing. Jesus Christ did not heal in Nazareth because the people lacked faith (Mark 6:5-6; Matthew 13:58). Also in Matthew 17:20, the disciples were told by Jesus that the reason that they could not cast out the demon was because they lacked faith. In James 5:16, the emphasis is on the prayer of faith that will provide healing.

Characteristics of Christ's healings were that they overruled the ordinary course of nature; they occurred instantaneously (Mark 1:42; 8:22-26) and were complete and permanent (Mark 5:27-29; Acts 5:15; 19:12). There were no relapses except when people were raised from the dead (Mark 5:21-24,35-43; Lk. 7:11-15; John 11:1-44). There are over 20 stories of healing in the

New Testament. The healing ministry of Jesus was shared by the 12 disciples on various occasions when he sent them away from his physical presence (Mark 6:7-13; Matthew 10:1-5; Luke 9:1-6) as well as when Christ sent out the 70 (Luke 10:9).

2. The purpose of healing:

If Christ's purpose on earth was to heal all the sick, there would have been more healing of people than what actually took place, and he probably would have healed everyone at the pool of Bethesda. Healing or any other miracles, whether in the Old or New Testament, were performed mostly to establish the leadership of someone or to authenticate the words spoken by that individual. Moses in Egypt became more believable, because God performed more miracles . David's kingship was established in the eyes of the people when he killed Goliath. Daniel was more respected when he came out unharmed from the lion's den. The same occurred for Shadrach, Meshach and Abed-nego.

When Christ came, there were more healings and or miracles in the early part of his ministry than in the latter part. The healings and/or miracles seemed to climax with the resurrection of Lazarus (John 11:43-44). His healings and/or miracles seemed to focus on illustrating the truth about what he was teaching. An example is when Christ fed the five thousand people (John 6). Later, he went on to teach "I am the bread" (John 6:35).

When Christ blessed Peter and his companions with a large catch of fish that miracle led Peter to follow Christ (Luke 5:1-11), Christ used it as an illustration to inform Peter that he would be fishing for men. When Christ healed the paralytic (Luke 5:17-26), he was teaching about the power of God to forgive sins. Jesus' healing on the Sabbath (John 7:19-22) is another example of this concept. Jesus clearly states this in John 10:37-38; "If I do not do the works of My Father, do not believe Me; but if I do them, though you do not believe Me, believe the works, so that you may know and understand that the Father is in Me, and I in the Father." This also demonstrates that the healings and miracles serve as signs that Jesus was the Christ "the Son of the Living God" (John 2:11; 5:36; 20:30-31).

The healings and/or miracles also assured the people that Jesus' message was a message from God; "this man came to him by night, and said to him, "Rabbi, we know that you have come from God as a teacher; for no one can do these signs that you do unless God is with him" (John 3:2). This is again confirmed in Acts 2:22: "Men of Israel, listen to these words: Jesus the Nazarene, a man attested to you by God with miracles and wonders and signs which God performed through him in your midst, just as you yourselves know..."

This very same thing occurred for the Apostles in Acts, which is reaffirmed in Hebrews 2:2-4. For the Apostles, the signs and wonders caused many unbelievers to believe in Christ. The church in Acts 2:42-45 continued to grow and was unified as a result of the signs and wonders. In Acts 8:5-8 "… Philip went down to the city of Samaria and began proclaiming Christ to them. And the multitudes with one accord were giving attention to what was said by Philip, as they heard and saw the signs that he was performing. For in the case of many who had unclean spirits, they were coming out of them shouting with a loud voice; and many who had been paralyzed and lame were healed, and there was much rejoicing in that city." This same thing took place in Acts 9:34-40,when Peter healed Aeneas miraculously by commanding him to get up "And all who lived at Lydda and Sharon saw him, and they turned to the Lord." The same thing took place in Acts 9:40-43 when Peter prayed for Tabitha that she would rise from the dead "And it became known all over Joppa, and many believed in the Lord."

In II Corinthians 12:12, Paul states "The signs of a true apostle were performed among you with all perseverance, by signs and wonders and miracles." In order to establish the Church and the authenticity of the disciples as Christ's followers and leaders, the Holy Spirit did many of the same miracles through the apostles that Christ did while he was with the disciples (Acts 3:1-11; 14:8-10; 9:3-34; 28:8; 5:15-16; 19:11-12; 16:16-18). As the Church and the apostles became more established, there were fewer healings and other miracles.

Paul healed the sick so powerfully that his "handkerchiefs or aprons" could be used to heal others. However, later in his ministry when Epaphroditus was close to death, Paul did not heal him through a miracle but prayed for him (Philippians 2:27-30). The same thing occurred with Timothy who had stomach complaints (I Timothy 5:23). Trophimus was too ill to accompany Paul from Miletus (II Timothy 4:20). Paul himself had a thorn in the flesh that Christ refused to heal (II Corinthians 12:7-10). It seems that the apostolic commission to heal could not be used indiscriminately to keep themselves or their friends free from illness. Miraculous healing was never used in these cases probably because these individuals were believers, not unbelievers.

These were people who already believed and did not need to be convinced of the power of Christ and the authenticity of the Word of God. Also, the Church was already established. This reinforces the point that miraculous healing was for the establishing of the Church and to stimulate the faith of the unbeliever. The need for the active presence of faith was obviously still important for healing (as it was when Christ performed miracles of healing; Hebrews 11:6). Therefore, in an established church, what James writes about in chapter 5:13-16 places more emphasis on faith and prayer than on signs and wonders. This need for faith, as it was with Christ, and the prayer of the righteous seem to have taken the place of the miraculous healings that occurred in the early developments of the New Testament Church.

C. Did miraculous healing start or stop with the Apostles?

While on earth, Christ performed three different kinds of miracles. There were healings (including raising people from the dead), casting out demons, and miracles of nature (like calming the sea, feeding the five thousands etc.). These were miraculous and they demonstrated tremendous powers (the word for miracle means power, which occurs 118 times in the New Testament). All miracles done by Christ were signs for leading everyone to believe that Jesus is God (John 2:11; 20:30-31; 5:36; 20:30-31; Acts 2:22).

The apostles never demonstrated that they had powers to do miracles of nature, but Christ gave them powers to cast out demons and "heal every kind of disease and every kind of sickness" (Matthew 10:1; Luke 9:1-2; 10:1-9). It seems that Christ limited these miraculous healings to his apostles focusing on winning the unsaved, and establishing their authority to lead the Church especially since the leaders of the Sanhedrin (Chief Priest, Pharisees, Scribes etc.) were telling people that Christ did not rise from the dead (II Corinthians 12:12; Mark 16:20; Hebrews 2:3,4). The only exceptions to this were Barnabas (Acts 15:12), Philip (Acts 8:7), and Stephen (Acts 6:8). We can clearly see this when Peter healed the lame man. Peter gained an audience immediately as a result of this miracle (Acts 4:4). These miracles were very similar to the ones that Jesus did; thereby proving that Jesus was alive through the apostles thus helping with the propagation of the gospel (Acts 3:2-8; 5:12-16; 9:32-35; 9:36-42; Acts 28).

However, this gift of healing did not seem to have been used by the apostles after the church was established at a time when many people had come to Christ. You do not find them healing the believers in the church miraculously. Epaphroditus in Philippians 2:25-27 was very sick, but Paul did not seek to heal him. The same occurred with Trophimus, who was sick at Miletus (II Timothy 4:20), and Timothy, himself in I Timothy 5:23. It is interesting to note that the charismatic churches teach that Christ wants all believers to be physically healthy although some sicknesses come from God (Exodus 4:11; II Corinthians 12:7; I Corinthians 11:30).

There is no record that anyone continued to heal miraculously after the apostles. It appears that God used this to win people to Christ and establish the New Testament Church through the ministry of the apostles, "how shall we escape if we neglect so great a salvation? After it was at the first spoken through the Lord, it was confirmed to us by those who heard, God also bearing witness with them, both by signs and wonders and by various miracles and by gifts of the Holy Spirit according to His own will" (Hebrews 2:3-4). Therefore, by the time of James (James 5:13-16), Christ was encouraging believers to use medicine (rubbing oil), and to pray always depending on God to provide healing. But when the sickness continues they must go to the elders for prayer. This does not mean that God cannot heal miraculously; I believe God no longer does it in the same manner that he did through Christ and the apostles (to be discussed more later).

D. An analysis of the words for healing as it was used in the New Testament:

There are three key words that are used for healing in the New Testament. They are "*therapeuo*" (to heal, serve), and "*iaomai*" (to cure, restore, to free from an evil), and "*sodei*" (preserve safe from danger, deliverance from disease). Of these three words, "*therapeuo*" exclusively means to heal. It is found 43 times in the New Testament. Of the 43 occurrences in the New Testament, it is found 40 of those times in the Synoptic Gospels and Acts. "*Therapeuo*" is used to describe Christ's two-fold ministry, which is "teaching" and "healing" (therapeuo Matthew 4:23; 9:35). The word is also used when Christ empowered the disciples to heal (therapeuo) the sick and cast out demons (Matthew 10:8; Mark 6:13; Luke 9:1).

The word ("therapeuo" and "iaomai") is used to represent God's work of healing, or restoring bodily or mental health (Matthew 9:35; 12:15). It is solely through the power and will of God that human well-being and good health can be restored fully. There is no need for therapy or medicine because it is a thorough restoration. The apostles and believers (Mark 9:38-41; Luke 9:49-50) were provided this healing power through Jesus Christ and the work of the Holy Spirit.

"Ia*omai*" occurs 26 times, of which 20 are in the Synoptic Gospels and Acts. The contextual meaning of "*iaomai*," in the Gospels and Acts, corresponds with that of "*therapeuo*." This takes place in Luke 9:2, when Christ empowered the disciples to heal the sick. However "*iaomai*" can refer to both physical and spiritual healing, whereas "*therapeuo*" refers primary to "care for the sick for the purpose of healing." This word, especially in its Old Testament context, views God as the only one who can heal.

However, "*sodei*" is used in James 5:15, which means, "to save, deliver, make whole, preserve safe from danger." It occurs 54 times in the Gospels (the number goes up in its occurrences elsewhere in the New Testament). In 14 of the 54 times in the Gospels it means "deliverance from disease or demon possession," to heal sick individuals, restore to health, (Matthew 9:21-22 "get well"; Mark 5:23,28,34; 6:56; 10:52; Luke 7:50; 8:36,48,50; 17:19; 18:42; John 11:12; Acts 4:9; James 5:15). In 20 instances, it refers to "rescue of physical life from some impending peril or instant death (Matthew 8:25; 14:30; 16:25; 27:40,42,49; Mark 8:35; 15:30,31; Luke 9:24,56; 23:35,37,39; John 12:27). In 20 other instances, it refers "to spiritual salvation" (there would be more occurrences elsewhere in the N.T. – Matthew 1:21; 10:22; 19:25; 24:13,22; Mark 8:35; 10:26; 13:13,20; 16:16; Romans 11:14; I Corinthians 1:21; I Timothy 4:16; Hebrews 7:25; James 1:21).

The basic meaning of this word is "to rescue from peril, to protect, keep alive." It also involves "preservation of life, either physical or spiritual," "healing from bodily infirmity." There are different words for healing so we must be careful how we interpret verses that contain the word "heal." We must pay close attention to the context of the passage, before interpreting the meaning of the verse.

II. Biblical Analysis Of James 5:13-16

A. An examination of the historical use of oil:

1. How was it made? The oil that was most frequently used came from the olive tree. Olives were harvested from September to October each year. After they were shaken or beaten off the branches (Deuteronomy 24:20; Isaiah 17:6), they were crushed either by treading, (Micah 6:15) by pestle and mortar, (Exodus 27:20; 29:40; Leviticus 24:2), or by grinding in a stone press (Joel 2:24). This was done mostly in Palestine.

2. What was it used for? Oil was used for several things. It was used for trade (I Kings 5:11; Ezra 3:7; Ezekiel 27:17), for food (I Kings 17:12-16; 2 Kings 4:2), for cosmetics (Ruth 3:3; II Samuel 14:2; Amos 6: 6; Matthew 6:17; Luke 7:46), for funerals where the deceased body was washed and anointed with oil, for light as was demonstrated in the parable of the foolish and wise virgins (Matthew 25:8; Luke 12:35), for medicinal purposes, which included internal use for gastric disorders or as a mild laxative, or externally as was demonstrated in the parable about the good Samaritan (Luke 10:34), for the consecrating of kings and priests (Exodus 29:7; I Samuel 10:1; I Kings 1:39), for ceremonial rituals such as the burnt offering (Exodus 29:40), the meal or gain offering (Leviticus 2:1-10), the Nazarene's offering (Numbers 6:15), the guilt offering of a clean leper (Leviticus 14:10-32), an offering of jealously (Numbers 5:15), and for tithes (Deuteronomy 12:17; II Chronicles 31:5; Nehe-

miah 10:37,39; 13:12; Ezekiel 45:14).

3. An important use that is significant for this study is that it was also used symbolically.

a. It symbolized the consecration and the endowment of the Holy Spirit (Leviticus 8:12; I Samuel 10:1,6; 16:13; Isaiah 61:1; Luke 4:18; Acts 10:38; II Corinthians 1:21).

b. It was used to symbolize joy, honor, and humiliation (Psalm 45:7; Isaiah 61:3; Joel 1:10; Hebrews 1:9). It was also used as an image of comfort, spiritual nourishment, or prosperity (Deuteronomy 33:24; Job 29:6; Psalm 45:7).

c. The olive tree symbolized the people of God (Romans 11:17-24), and is mentioned in Revelation 11:4 as two witnesses that "will prophesy for 1,260 days, clothed in sackcloth."

d. It was used for the anointing of the tabernacle, its furnishings, the ark of the testimony, kings, and Aaron and his sons (Exodus 30:22-33; Exodus 29:7; I Samuel 10:1; 1 Kings1:39).

e. Jesus seems to have used the Mt. of Olivet, where the olive tree grew, for teaching and for his ascension to heaven (Luke 24:50-51;

Acts 1:12).

f. The disciples used it to symbolize miraculous healing (Mark. 6:13; James 5:14).

4. Oil is use in James 5:14:

The oil in James was not used for med icinal reasons because it was directly placed on a wound. It can also be used symbolically to reinforce faith, as Christ did when he used clay or spittle to heal the blind man (Mark 7:33; 8:23; John 9: 6). Mixing spit with dirt was viewed as a form of medicine for healing disease in the eye. Jesus obviously did not depend on this for healing, but may have used it to reinforce the man's faith. Jesus consistently emphasized faith when he performed miraculous healing (review page 48). In the same way, oil used in James 5:14 can serve to reinforce the faith of the believers since the emphasis in the passage is faith and the power of prayer.

B. Historical use of the word "Anointing":

1. Anointing gained symbolic and religious recognition before Christ came to earth. Many people in the ancient world believed that anytime, anyone became sick it was because the gods were mad at them. Therefore by anointing them, they would rid the person of the angry god or de-

mons. It was seen as magical in Egypt (this is probably where the Israelites got it from), and in Babylon. It waslater used for the care of the body, and cometics.It was always viewed as providing healing or refreshment for the body.

2. It was customary to anoint the heads of important guests, but the host would provide only water for their feet (example Mary in John 12:1-11).

3. The corpse was first anointed with oil then washed with water except for criminals who sometimes may have been denied anointing before burial (though not Jesus; John 19:39-40).

4. Anointing was usually a mark of festivity. Its omission was an act of discourtesy towards a guest (Luke 7:46). When men were engaged in solemn activities such as fasting, they sometimes refrained from anointing as a way of drawing attention to what they were doing a practice which Jesus discouraged (Matthew 6:16). Anointing was thus associated with revelry more than with funerals (Proverbs 27:9; Daniel 10:3; II Samuel 14:2).

5. Anointing with oil was also used for healing by means of the oil (Psalm 23:5; 45:7; Ecclesiastes 9:8; Isaiah 1:6; Ezekiel 16:9; Luke 10:34,38; John 19:40).

6. Anointing with oil was also used for anointing the tabernacle furniture, priests, kings (Exodus 30:26; 40:10; Leviticus 4:3,5; I Samuel 16:13), etc.

C. A word study of anoint:

There are two primary words that are used for anoint "*chrio*" and "*aleipho*". We'll examine these words separately and summarize their differences.

Chrio:

Means to anoint or to smear over. It has a sacred sense, meaning to anoint symbolically. The name Christ comes from "*chrio*," to anoint (Psalm 45:7; Hebrews 1:9. This emphasizes the sacred meaning of this word and is consistently translated to anoint (Luke 4:18; Acts 4:27; 10:38; II Corinthians 1:21).

Aleipho: this is the word used in James (aleipsantes - aor. act. part.):

Means to rub in, or smear on. This was the rubbing with oil focused on providing healing. It was a medicinal means of healing as seen with the Samarian man on the road to Jericho (Luke 10:30-37).

This word is seldom used ceremonially. In Mark 6:17 it is used to encourage those who are fasting to refresh themselves. This word is also used to care for the dead (Mark 16:1; Luke 23:56; John 19:40). The rubbing on of oil was used to slow down the decaying process and reduce the odor of the decaying body.

This word was also used for the honoring of guests (Luke 7:38,46; John 11:2; 12:3). This word was used when Jesus was anointed by the sinful woman (Luke 7:38) as a point to the Pharisees who failed to anoint their guest.

D. Anoint as it relates to James 5:14:

Jesus in Mark 6:13, and James in James 5:14, used "*aleipho*" because he seemed to focus on the use of oil as a medicine to be joined with prayer, as compared with "*chrio*,", which is specifically used for sacred anointing. Therefore, along with someone going to the doctor, (viewing this within our context) we should gather the elders together to pray so that along with the normal use of medicine; God will perform a miracle. Believers are not to put their faith in the medicine, but in God through prayer. This was the emphasis for Paul's healing of the father of Publius in Acts 28:8. A similar case occurred in Acts 9:40. The emphasis again was on prayer. Hence along with oil, which was used in the same way that Jesus used water and dirt (John 9:6-7), the person being healed must place his faith in Jesus Christ as the person prays.

The emphasis in this passage (James 5:14) was not on the anointing with oil but on prayer. Prayer is the main verb, while anoint is a participle. Prayer is mentioned in verse 13, and repeated in verse 14,15, and 16. Prayer is highlighted again in verse 17 and 18 with the prayer of Elijah for God to stop the rain. This example was used to emphasize that Elijah's prayer as a righteous man accomplished much.

E. An examination of the word "sick":

There are two words that James uses for "sick." They are "*astheneo*" (pres. act. ind.), and "*kamno*" (pres. act. ptc. acc. sing. masc.).

Astheneo: This word means to be sick or weak. It can refer to a special form of bodily weakness or sickness, i.e. those suffering from physical, psychosomatic, emotional, or whatever causes a person to state, "I don't feel well." It can refer to physical weaknesses due to specific diseases. An example of this is Jesus' statement about Lazarus death. Jesus said, "This sickness (astheneia) is not unto death" (John 11:4). The same thing occurs in Acts 9:37, "And it came about at that time that she fell sick and died ... ." This was a weakness or sickness that led to death.

Some other examples are found in Romans 8:26, I Corinthians 2:3, and seven times in the Gospels. The most significant occurrence is in Matthew 8:17, which is a quotation of Isaiah 53:4 that states that Christ took on our weakness which represented our sin nature. In I Corinthians 2:3, it seems to refer to timidity, or lack of strength or power. Another occurrence is I Corinthians 15:43, which refers to the bodies corruptibility or weakness. In II Corinthians 11:30; 12:5,9,10, Paul speaks of his weaknesses referring to the results of Adamic sin, which in no way should overwhelm the believer because God is able (Romans 4:20; Ephesians 6:10; Philippians 4:13; I Timothy 1:12; II Timothy 2:1;4:17).Other references for use of the word are II Corinthians 11:21; Romans 4:1; 14:2,21; I Corinthians 8:9,11,12.

Sometimes the word seems to refer directly to a sickness or disease. In Acts 28:9, the word can mean diseases, or ailments. Another reference is I Timothy 5:23. Concerning the man who had a physical ailment or disease, the Apostles made reference to his sickness when they responded to the Pharisees "if we are on trial today for a benefit done to the sick ("*astheneo*") man, as to how this man has been made well" (Acts 3:6; 4:9). Another account of this is in I Corinthians 11:30. The word weakness is mentioned, but it seems to be a reference to a sickness inflicted by God as an act of judgment due to the flagrant abuse of the Lord's Supper. Other occurrences of this particular meaning of the word are found in Matthew 10:8; 25:36; Mark 6:56; Luke 4:40; 7:10.

Kamno:

Means to be weary from constant work (Hebrews 12:3; Job 10:1). However, when it is used in connection with "*astheneo*," it can mean to be sick, or that the weariness of the mind can hinder physical recovery.

Kakopathei:

This word means to suffer misfortune, hardship, suffering evil, or bearing affliction (James 5:10,13; II Timothy 1:8). In summary, "*astheneo*" means sick or weak, "*kamno*" means to be sick or weary, and "*kakopathei*" means to suffer personal distress.

F. An examination of word for "raised" (*egerei*):

Egerei

This word means to rise up from a sick bed to health (Matthew 2:9), to rise up from a sleep, to rise up from reclining at a table, and to help a person who is unable to stand, to stand on his feet.

III. General Observations Based On The Information Provided Above For James 5:13-16

Because James attaches "*sodei*," (will heal) and "*aleipho*," (having anointed) in this passage it seems that James is speaking about physical healing not emotional suffering as some commentators advocate. He also mentions the need for faith in verse 15, which was an important ingredient when Christ was physically healing on earth.

Notice that James mentions the word "sodei" (will heal) twice, once in verse 14, and again in verse 15. James makes a distinction between sickness and suffering in verse 13 and 14; "Is anyone among you suffering? Let him pray" (vs. 13). Notice anyone in the congregation may pray for this individual who is suffering from misfortune, hardship, suffering evil, or bearing affliction (vs. 13). The same thing occurs in verse 16; anyone who is righteous should pray for those who have committed sins (notice the contrast, sins of one individual compared to a person who is praying for restoration from suffering; this person is righteous (Galatians 6:1).

However, when James mentions "Is anyone among you sick?" (vs. 14, using both "*astheneo*" and "*kamno*" in the present tense, meaning who continues to be sick), the elders of the church were to be called, and this is also where we find the word "*aleipho*" (having anointed) mentioned along with the use of oil. It is not mentioned for the person who is suffering or the person who has committed sins; probably since the oil is used as a healing agent in this passage (*chrio* is not used – the word for sacred anointing). The person with sins or the person suffering would obviously not need it. Regarding the person who is sick, verse 16 states, "the Lord will raise them." The word raise (*egerie*) means "raise from the bed of sickness to health." This is not mentioned for the person who is suffering in verse 13 or the person who is healed from sin in verse 16. Since "*astheneo*" (is sick or weak) is mentioned along with "*aleipho*" (having anointed), and the anointing of oil is medicinal, it seems likely that James is discussing the healing of a physical ailment or disease that is persistent.

IV. Summary Of The Views Of Commentators

A. R.V.G. Tasker: Tyndale New Testament Commentaries

"The purpose of the use by the elders of oil in the name of the Lord, as they prayed over the sick man, was we might assume, the same as the use by the apostles of the laying-on of hands. It helped in certain cases by the application of a substance that could be felt by the patient to reinforce the evidence of the ear that the Lord was being invoked by the prayer of faith to bestow upon him, if it should be His will, a miraculous cure: Moreover, the emphasis on "in the name of the Lord" made it clear that, if a cure was effected, it was the Lord's doing and not man's."

"The meaning seems to be that, if God should effect a miraculous cure in answer to the elders' prayer of faith accompanied by anointing with oil in the name of the Lord, that would be a clear indication that any sins of the sufferer, which might have been responsible for this particular illness, were forgiven. It was the sight of the paralytic taking up his mattress and walking that provided unmistakable evidence that his sins, which had clearly resulted in his affliction, really had been forgiven."

B. Peter Davids: New International Greek Testament Commentary on James:

"It is true that "*astheneo*" (sick or weak) may indicate weakness of any form (e.g. 4:19; I Corinthians 8:9; II Corinthians 11:29; BAG, 114, for other meanings), but the contrast with "*kakopathei*" (suffer ill), the need to call the elders to him, the use of oil, and the two terms "*sodei*" (will heal) and "*kumvonid*" (being sick) indicate that illness is intended." (Page 192.) "It is God's power (i.e. "*o kurios*" in 5:15) which will heal the person. Thus one finds three actions in the healing rite: prayer, anointing, and the calling out of the name of Jesus." "The term "prayer" naturally sums up the whole action of 5:14, keeping the stress of the verse on prayer. It is a prayer of faith, i.e. the prayer, which expresses trust in God and flows out of commitment to him, for only such prayers are effective (James 1:5-8; Mark 2:5; 5:34; 10:52; 6:6; Acts 14:9, where faith or lack of it is the condition for healing). The faith is that of the one who prays, i.e. of the elders who have ex officio healing power, not that of the sick person (who may or may not be in a condition to exercise much of anything)." (Page 194)

C. Frank E. Gaebelien: The Expositors Bible Commentary:

"Prayer is more significant of the two ministries performed by the elders. "Pray, is the main verb, while "anoint" is a participle. Moreover, the overall emphasis of the paragraph is on prayer. So the anointing is a secondary action. There are a number of reasons for understanding this application of oil as medicinal rather than sacramental. The word "*aleipsantes*" (anoint) is not the usual word for sacramental or ritualistic anointing. James could have used the verb "*chrio*" if that had been what he had in mind. The distinction is still observed in Modern Greek, with "*aleipho*" meaning "to daub," "to smear," and "*chrio*" meaning "to anoint." Furthermore, it is a well-documented fact that oil was one of the most common medicines of biblical times." (Page 203-204)

D. Douglas J. Moo: Tyndale New Testament Commentaries:

"When the elders come, they are to pray over (*epi*) the one who is sick. Only here in biblical Greek is *proseuchomai* (pray) followed by epi: it may simply indicate physical position, but could possibly imply that hands were also laid on the sick person (Matthew 19:13)." (Pages 176-177)

"Oil was widely used in the ancient world as a medicine (Luke 10:34). Other ancient sources attest to its helpfulness is curing everything from toothache to paralysis (the hamous second-centtury physician Galen recommended oil as 'the best of all remedies for paralysis', Mod. Temp. 2). What James may be saying, then, is that the elders should come to the bedside of the sick armed with both spiritual and natural resources-with prayer and with medicine. Both are administered with the Lord's authority and both together can be used by him in healing the sick." (Page 177)

"As a different kind of practical purpose, others suggest that the anointing may have been intended as an outward, physical expression of concern and as a means to stimulate the faith of the sick person. Jesus sometimes used physical 'props' in his healing, apparently with just such a purpose. But when Jesus did so the physical action was specifically appropriate to the illness such as rubbing the eyes of a blind man (Mark 8:23-26) and placing his finger in the ears of a deaf man (Mark 7:33). There is simply no evidence that anointing with oil was generally used with such a purpose." (Page 178)

"On the other hand, the fact that anointing a sick person is mentioned only here in the New Testament epistles, and that many healings were accomplished without anointing, shows that the practice is not a necessary accompaniment to the prayer for healing. Elders who pray for the sick may do it, and James clearly recommends the practice; but they do not have to do so." (Page 179) "It is best, to view James' anointing as a physical action with symbolic significance. Since the symbolism of 'anointing' is usually associated with the setting apart or consecrating of someone or something for God, we are probably to understand this as the symbolism intended in the action. As the elders prayer for the sick person, they also set that person apart for God's special attention." (Page 181)

"A more helpful observation is to note James' specific reminder that the prayer must be a prayer of faith. This faith, while certainly including the notion of confidence in God's ability to answer, also involves absolute confidence in the perfection of God's will. Therefore, the 'faith' that is the indispensable condition for our prayers for healing to be answered - this faith being the gift of God - can be truly present only when it is God's will to heal." (Page 182)

"While *astheneo* (sick, weak) can denote spiritual weakness, this meaning is usually made clear by a qualifier (Romans 14:2, 'in faith'; I Corinthians 8:7, 'in conscience') or the context. Moreover, in the material that is most relevant to James, the

Gospels, *astheneo* almost always refers to illness. The same is true for *kamno* (sick, weary). And "*iaomai*," when not used in an Old Testament quotation, always refers in the New Testament to physical healing. Beyond this, it is significant that the only other mention of 'anointing with oil' in the New Testament comes in a description of physical healing (Mark 6:13)." (Page 184)

Conclusion And Summary Of The Meaning Of The Text:

James expects the sick individuals in the church, who continue to be sick, to go to the elders for prayer. Elders must exercise faith, and believe in the name of the Lord in order for these individuals to be healed. Oil is used as a healing agent in the text, which in our context could mean the use of a doctor or medicine. It is quite obvious that Christ did not see anything wrong with a believer going to a doctor (Matthew 9:12). Hence, along with the medicinal support, and the prayers of the elders which is done with faith, the believer can be physically healed as a result of the power of Jesus Christ.

7

Lord's Supper

Purpose Of This Chapter:

The purpose of this chapter is to first establish the significance of the Lord's Supper in biblical history then establish its function in the New Testament Church.

A. Historical Background:

1. The Old Testament festivals and sacrifices were often connected to meals that involved eating and drinking before God (Genesis 31:46, 54; Exodus 18:12; 24:11). It was called the Table-Fellowship meal.

2. The Table-Fellowship meal bonded those participating together in the presence of God, making them brothers to one another as well as sealing a covenant between them. To break this covenant was the most detestable of crimes. (Jeremiah 41:1; Psalm 41:9).

3. The Table Fellowship meant the granting of:

    a) The beginning and the thanksgiving at the end of the Passover meal.

    b) Forgiveness (2 Samuel 9:7; 2 Kings 25:27-30).

    c) Protection (Judges 19:15).

    d) Peace (Genesis 43:25).

    e) Agreement

    f) Fellowship

4. This meal, for the Jews under the Mosaic covenant, became the Passover meal signifying the freedom from slavery in Egypt symbolized by the blood on the doorpost. The blood typified Christ's death setting us free from slavery to sin. The Lord's Supper was held during the Passover and represented the Passover meal (Mark 14:12,14,16; Luke 22: 7,11,12,15).

5. This Table-Fellowship continued to the time of Christ. Christ did this with his disciples, tax collectors and sinners (this is why many Jewish leaders were upset. Matthew 9:9-13; Mark 2:13-17; Luke 5:27-32), as well as the feeding of the five thousand (Matthew 14:13-32; Mark 6:30-44; Luke 9:10-17; John 6:1-13). In these meetings, Jesus was

providing forgiveness and peace to his participants.

B. Theological Significance (Matthew 26:26-29; Mark 14: 22-25; Luke 22:15-20; I Corinthians 11:23-25; Acts 2:42, 46; 20:7, 11):

1. The Lord's Supper is sometimes called the Holy Communion or the Eucharist, and it serves as one of two ordinances along with baptism.

2. Jesus was the Passover lamb. This is why the meal took place during the Passover and Jesus did not return to Bethany where he normally spent the night (Matthew 21:17; 26:6; Mark 11:11; Mark 11:19; 14:3). He stayed in Jerusalem, the Holy City. There was a rule that the Passover lamb must be eaten within the city limits.

3. He was the Lamb, and is referred to many times in the O.T. and N.T. as the Lamb (Isaiah 53:7; John 1:29; Acts 8:32; I Corinthians 5:7; I Peter 1:19; Revelation 5:6,12; 19:9; 21:23).

4. Christ said that he is the bread which represents his body (probably a reference to Isaiah 53), and the wine represented his blood. Also he said, as recorded by John in chapter 6 verse 53 "... *I say to you, unless you eat the flesh of the Son of Man and drink His blood, you have no life in yourselves.*"

a) Paul viewed the bread as "one loaf" (I Corinthians 10:16-17), which signified the body of Christ. The body of Christ is represented as a community of believers functioning together as one. This is an important principle because Christ prayed for the Church to function in unity (John 17:20-23).

b) It seems as if the N.T. church used the bread quite often (Matthew 26:26; Luke 24:30,35; Acts 2:42,46; 20:7,11; I Corinthians 11:20, 23-28). This could be because of the following:

i) When Christ gave the command for them to eat the Lord's Supper, he used bread as reprepresenting his body and the wine as representing his blood (Luke 22:18-21).

ii) Christ referred to himself as the Bread of Life (John 6:35-40, 50-58) and viewed the bread as representing His body (Matthew 26:26; Mark 14:22; Luke 22:19).

iii) The Passover meal is represented in the Lord Supper. Christ celebrates this meal on the day of the unleavened bread (Matthew 26:17; Mark 14:12; Luke 22:1,7).

iv) Jesus used bread when he along with his disciples participated in the Lord's Supper (Luke 24:30,35).

v) Paul viewed one loaf of bread as portraying the body of Christ, which highlights unity in the Church (I Corinthians 10:16-17).

5. The Lord's Supper based on the passages mentioned above means:

a) Fellowship meal - the fellowship of the believers.

b) An assurance of forgiveness of sins.

c) Participation in God's order of salvation (sharing in the sacrifice of Christ, like the Jews shared in the Passover symbolically), and incorporation into a new covenant.

d) That it was a time of accountability for believers to maintain purity (I Corinthians 11:23-34).

e) "The proclamation of the incarnation of the Logos, in which the Son's self-offering is accomplished."

f) Because of the purification process and the fellowship of believers, the Lord's Supper had a built-in theological basis for unity.

g) "In remembrance of me" (I Corinthians 11:24-25, this is a command) signifies that the the Lord's Supper is a remembrance of Christ's death. However, it is not a re-enactment. It declares a historical event that is the center of the Christian faith.

h) It has eschatological significance; "... you proclaim the Lord's death until he comes" (I Corinthians 11:26). Also, the hope to participate in the heavenly feast for a thousand years with Christ (Revelation 21).

i) It is essential to the proclamation of the Gospel message of I Corinthians 11:26: " ... You proclaim the Lord's death ... ."

6. The Lord's Supper also represented the final Messianic banquet (Isaiah 25:6; Luke 14:15-24) when the divine work of salvation is consummated and there is a fulfillment of fellowship with the Lord (Matthew 26:29).

7. Key reasons for participating in the Lord's Supper:

   a) It is in remembrance of Christ (I Corinthians 11:24).

   b) It is a proclamation of his death (I Corinthians 11:26).

c) It is assurance of Christ's Second Coming (Matthew 26:29; 1 Corinthians 11:26).

d) It is a time of fellowship with Christ and his people (I Corinthians 10:21).

C. Purpose of the Lord's Supper:

The Lord's Supper served as a reminder of the central importance of the death of Jesus as a sacrifice for his people, providing them a new everlasting covenant (making the old covenant obsolete) with the Father, and meaning in the proclamation of the Gospel message. This is essential for genuine worship because worship consists of fellowship with each other as a result of fellowship with God, prayer, salvation, and edification. All of these elements of worship can flourish as a result of believers actively participating in the Lord's Supper. The Lord's Supper serves as the core from which everything evolves.

D. The Meaning of the Elements:

The bread represents Christ body, which was pierced (broken is probably pointing back to Isaiah 53). It also represents Christ's flesh (John 6:51-53).

The wine (fruit of the vine Israel viewed itself as a vine, which was symbolic for life. Christ is now the true vine Luke 22:18; John 15:1, representing a new life that will last forever) - represents Christ's blood (the vine pro duces wine) signifying a new covenant for Jews and Gentiles. This means salvation for the believer, and is symbolic of the blood on the doorpost of the Jews who were departing from Egypt under Moses' leadership.

The cup (means the usual cup) - signifies blessing and thanksgiving. It contains the blood (wine), which seals the covenant, "this cup is the new covenant in my blood." It was the cup of blessing that the honored guest lifted up when giving the benediction.

E. Practical Application for the N.T. Church:

1. It should occur during worship service.

2. Several things must occur before the Lord's Supper is served. They are as follows:

   a) Believers should seek to purify themselves before God. This can occur through prayer seeking God's forgiveness so that we draw near to him in full assurance with a clear conscience (Hebrews 10:19-22).

   b) Believers must seek to be in fellowship with each other representing their genuine fellowship with God, and unity in the body.

   c) Non-Christians must not be allowed to participate.

d) Believers must be reminded of the biblical significance of this process.

F. How often should The Lord's Supper be served?

Paul states in 1 Corinthians 11:25, *"This cup is the new covenant in My blood; do this, as often as you drink it, in remembrance of Me."* In Acts 2:46 Luke states *"And day by day continuing with one mind in the temple, and breaking bread from house to house."* Often means "much, many, many times." Robertson and Plummer state that this is a command and "that the Supper be often repeated, and his Apostle charges those who repeat it to keep in view of him who instituted it, and who died to give life to them." The Greek translation of often used with "*ean*" means "every time." The usual construction used to denote repetition.

It could be that the reason why Paul stated this, is to emphasize the need to do this consistently in a church that was out of order. The consistency may have assisted the church in regaining unity and genuine worship. There seems to be a consistent practice, in the churches in Acts, to have the Lord's Supper every week. Here are the passages:

1. Acts 20:7; *"And on the first day of the week, when we were gathered together to break bread, Paul {began} talking to them, intending to depart the next day, and he prolonged his message until midnight."*

2. Acts 2:42; *"And they were continually devoting themselves to the apostles' teaching and to fellowship, to the breaking of bread and to prayer."*

3. Since the Lord's Supper is done to remember him, and we gather because of him (the one who saved us) to worship him, the Lord's Supper should be celebrated each time worship occurs. Christ commanded us to do this in remembrance of him. *"And when He had taken{some bread} {and} given thanks, He broke {it,} and gave {it} to them, saying, "This is my body which is given for you;* ***do this*** *in remembrance of Me."* (Luke 22:19)

Summary:

It is obvious based on this study that the Lord's Supper must (must, because it is a command) be done either every time like the believers in Acts or many times, meaning regularly. However based on the Greek construction of the phase it seems to be every time. Believers are commanded to participate, and they must highlight the true significance of the Supper.

8

The Lottery And Its Social Impact

Introduction

In this chapter, we will only examine how the Word of God responds to believers playing the lottery. Politicians knew that it would be most unpopular to raise taxes so they encouraged voters to accept the lottery as a means to an end. The lottery basically is paying voluntary taxes at the expense of the poor and our youth. The Detroit News reports that "low-income, inner-city residents clinging to dreams of jackpots and instant fortunes are among the Michigan State Lottery's best customers."

A 1988 study of the Michigan lottery showed that the state government "sells the greatest number of lottery tickets in low-income predominantly black neighborhoods in urban areas." It was also found that most of the advertisement in Michigan was aimed at poor blacks hoping to get rich quickly. Alan Karcher, the House Speaker for New Jersey, states that "it is highly unlikely that a person will hear lottery commercials on a classical music station or read one in the Wall Street Journal, but highly likely to find a lottery advertisement on a poster on an inner-city bus or in papers printed in Spanish. Advertising is focused on fantasy, attacks the work ethic, is timed to encourage heavy participation by those on social security, and is targeted to the poor." In a suburban section of Michigan where 63 percent of the residents were educated whites, the lottery was a bust.

The lottery exploits the poor, who have little or no chance of winning. Clearly these facts do not even address the effects on the low-income family, whose money is now being spent on something else that provides little or no return. The issue of the effects of lottery on crime is not even being addressed as well.

I. Sociological Impact:

The lottery was not for the benefit of the poor, but mostly for the government which finds it difficult to control its spending, because of the influence of many special interest groups. Playing the lottery will not only exploit the poor; it will also enslave our youth. Valerie Lorenz, director of the National Center for Pathological Gambling states: "The lottery created a dramatic rise in youth gambling," and "compulsive gambling is a progressive illness and lotteries encourage young people to start." Studies show that most compulsive gamblers start gambling between ages 13 and 18. Arnold Wexler, Director, J.J. Council on Compulsive Gambling states that "the lottery is the first step."

Dr. J. Henderson, executive director of the Georgia Council on Moral and Civic Concerns states, "A decade ago, teenage gambling failed to register a blip on the social-problem screen. Today, over seven million American youths gamble. One million have serious gambling problems more than a third began gambling before they were 15." The biggest problem is that most of our kids see this form of gambling as acceptable. Sirgay Sanger, president of the National Council on Compulsive Gambling, states that young people view gambling "as a readily available and attractive alternative if alcohol and drugs become less popular."

Howard Shaffer of the Center for Addiction Studies states, "We will face more problems with youth gambling than with illicit drug use." Dr. Durand Jacob, a University Psychologist relays his study of four lottery states, which showed that half of the high school students gambled and 13 percent of the students use what they had won to finance their gambling with crimes. It is ironic that the lottery which was supposed to enhance the education of our youth now serves to inflict wounds in their lives.

Christ states in Matthews 18:6, *"But if anyone causes one of these little ones who believe in me to sin, it would be better for him to have a large millstone hung around his neck and to be drowned in the depths of the sea."* Christians, the lottery is another one of Satan's schemes; it is not the answer to your financial or personal woes. Better financial planning, becoming better trained, and living godly is the best long-term investment you can make.

II. Old Testament Overview:

Playing the lottery is gambling. It is depending on luck or chance to provide extra income. This is addressed in Isaiah 65:11 (NIV) where he denounces the Israelites for being influenced by pagan religions and customs, *"But as for you who forsake the Lord and forget my holy mountain, who spread a table for Fortune, and who fill cups with mixed wine for Destiny."* Notice the word Fortune and Destiny are capitalized in the verse. This is because these were pagan gods of luck and chance. These gods were also viewed as mystical, fictitious powers that pagans believed could bestow good and evil.

It was a religion of the Hittites and Amorites. Playing at the "table of fortune" meant that a person was participating in an ancient religious practice of divination to foretell the future or a way to discover hidden knowledge by magic or supernatural means for determining their destiny. This is the reason God became angry at Saul (I Samuel 28:7-19). What this does is take us back to what occurred in the Garden of Eden. In the Garden of Eden, Satan told Eve by eating the fruit she would discover a hidden knowledge that would make her as powerful and as resourceful as God.

It is the same game that is advertised to get us to play the lottery. If you win the lottery, you can strike it rich and be in control of your own destiny, and your worries will be over. Maybe you will not need to work anymore, thereby becoming your own boss. It is not a game of lottery that our government is selling us. It is the primitive religion of the Hittites and Amorites which finds its place in Satan as demonstrated in the Garden of Eden. Isaiah was not mad at the Israelites for worshiping the Hittite and Amorite gods as much as he was upset that they allowed themselves to become a part of the service by playing the "tables of Fortune." Christians forget that *"our struggle is not against flesh and blood, but against the rulers, against the authorities against the powers of this dark world and against the spiritual forces of evil in the heavenly realms"* (Ephesians 6:12 NIV). Proverbs provides us many reasons why is it not profitable for a believer to play the lottery as a means of caring for his family or for getting rich (Proverbs 12:11; 13:11; Proverbs 28:19-20). Proverbs clearly states that God will punish someone who seeks to get-rich-quick.

III. New Testament Overview:

I understand that at times when finances are a problem, or we need a financial boost, winning a lot of money can seem like a blessing from heaven. However, because a Christian is a born again believer, the question should always be "What does my heavenly Father, heavenly Governor and heavenly Legislator have to say about the issue? Where does he cast his vote?" Fortunately God does not take sides.

His Word is truth, so for him it is never a matter of how much sense or "no sense" the lottery makes. It is the Word of God that provides us direction. So, it is the duty of a believer to evaluate how the Word of God addresses the issue. The Bible does not encourage quick get-rich schemes because it violates the work ethic by promoting "something for nothing".

II Thessalonians 3:10 states, *"For even when we were with you we gave you the rule: 'If a man will not work, he shall not eat.'"* Verse 12 states, *"Such people we command and urge in the Lord Jesus Christ to settle down and earn the bread they eat."* Also in I Thessalonians 4:11 Paul states, *"Make it your ambition to lead a quiet life, to mind your own business and to work with your hands, just as we told you."* It's not that God does not want us to be prosperous; it is just that his focus is different as stated in Matthew 6:19, *"Do not store up for yourselves treasure on earth, where moth and rust destroy, and where thieves break in and steal."*

Don't become so caught up in being rich that you sell your soul to Satan (James 4:4; I John 2:15-17). I Timothy 6:9 says, *"People who want to get rich fall into temptation and a trap and into many foolish and harmful desires that plunge men into ruin and destruction."* Also see Proverbs 28:19-20; 12:11. Even to those who are rich, Paul states in I Timothy 6:17,18, *"Command those who are rich in this present world not to be arrogant nor to put their hope in wealth, which is so uncertain, but to put their hope in God, who richly provides us with everything for our enjoyment."* If you argue that in an economy like ours, it helps to play the lottery, then you have made a decision to let the "table of fortune"; the table of luck or chance be your provider.

The Bible clearly states in Matthew 6:24, that "No one can serve two masters. Either he will hate the one and love the other, or he will be devoted to the one and despise the other. <u>You cannot</u> serve both God and Money." This is why God states in Luke 12:15 when he was talking about the rich man, "watch out! Be on your <u>guard against all kinds of greed; a man's life does not consist of the abundance of his possessions.</u>" And Paul states, "for the love of money, it is a root of all kinds of evil. <u>Some people eager for money, have wandered from the faith and pierce themselves with many griefs</u>" (I Timothy 6:10).

What the lottery teaches us directly conflicts with the Word of God, therefore, "Set your minds on the things above not on earthly thing, for you died, and your life in now hidden with Christ in God" (Colossians 3:2-3). Our present needs should never serve to tarnish our future glorification or living a Christ-centered life in this present world. The Word of God teaches us to seek Christ first: "But seek first His kingdom, and these things shall be added to you ... For where your treasure is, there will your heart be also" (Luke 12:31,34). "The kingdom of heaven is like treasure hidden in a field. When a man found it, he hid it again, and then in his joy went and sold all he had and bought that field" (Matthew 13:44).

Based on the evidence provided above, a Christian must not participate in this religion, and allow themselves to become involved in get rich quick schemes. This violates God's Word and causes Christians to shift their loyalty and trust from God to money. I challenge all Christians to focus their lives upon the living Word of God, so that you can be a light to this dark world.

9

The Church Accepting Gifts From Non-Biblical Means

Introduction

This issue attacks our moral convictions as well as our desire to discourage believers from gaining money by non-biblical means. As a pastor, I also struggle with the concern that money acquired by means that violate God's Word can be used to minister to people encouraging them to live moral lives. This can cause our ministry to seem questionable in the minds of unbelievers and believers. This is important because it is our testimony in the community that allows Christ to be honored or dishonored.

Even though these concerns are legitimate, they should not impede our desire to find the mind of Christ concerning this matter. After we have developed a biblical understanding of this issue, then we must seek to find ways to apply God's answer for his glory and honor.

An Explanation of the Problem

The issue is very simple. It can be addressed by answering two questions: **Can the church take money from individuals who are unbelievers? Can the church take money from believers or unbelievers who gamble, sell drugs or practice any vice that violates God's Word?**

I. Money From Unbelievers

A. How this subject is addressed relative to Israel:

1. After Abraham rescued Lot one-tenth of Lot's property and one-tenth of the defeated kings' property was given to God's priest (Genesis 14:13-20). Abraham however, did not accept any gifts from the King of Sodom (Genesis 14:21-24 – Abraham gave back to the King of Sodom his share) even though he accepted gifts from the Pharaoh of Egypt (Genesis 12:14-13:1).

   Abraham did not accept the property of the Sodomites because he said that he did not want them to take credit for making him wealthy.

2. There are three occurrences in the Bible where the nation of Israel benefited from unbelievers (Non-covenanted Gentiles):

a) When Israel was leaving Egypt, they were told to take articles of silver and gold from the Egyptians that were to be used for the building of the Ark of the Covenant (Exodus 3:22; 12:35-36; 25:1-9).

b) When Israel went into the promised land and settled in it, they used what the Gentiles left; they did not tear down the Gentile's homes (Joshua 8:27; 11:14; 13:6-7).

c) When Cyrus was moved by God to send Israel back to rebuild the temple, he assisted them with articles of silver and gold etc., to rebuild the temple (Ezra 1; II Chronicles 36: 21-23). The people of Israel used this to buy timber from Lebanon (Ezra 3:7).

3. After he was vindicated from Haman's wicked attempt to destroy the Jews, Mordecai accepted everything the King gave him that belonged to Haman and used it (Esther 8:4,10).

4. Achan was not allowed to keep property of the Amorites. It seems that God responded in this manner because he did not want the people coveting the Amorites wealth. God wanted them to trust him to make them wealthy.

Amorites

Shortly before 2000 B.C., the Amorites lived in the wilderness regions of what today is western Saudi Arabia and southern Syria. In the court records of ACCAD and SUMER they were known as barbarians, or uncivilized people. Beginning about 2000 B.C., the Amorites migrated eastward to Babylon in large numbers. There they captured major cities and regions from the native Mesopotamians. (Nelson's Illustrated Bible Dictionary.)

Much of our knowledge about the Amorites and their culture comes from clay tablets discovered at MARI, a major Amorite city situated on the Euphrates River in western Mesopotamia. (From Nelson's Illustrated Bible Dictionary.)

B. Bible passages that address this issue:

1. Deuteronomy 8:17-18; "Otherwise, you may say in your heart, 'My power and the strength of my hand made me this wealth.' But you shall remember the LORD your God, for it is He who is giving you power to make wealth, that He may confirm His covenant which He swore to your fathers as {it is} this day." (Another similar passage is Psalm 105:37; I Chronicles 29:12). God views all wealth as coming from him. The Israel ites received property from the Egyptians when they were leaving Egypt.

2. Psalm 49:10; "For he sees {that even} wise men die; the stupid and the senseless alike perish, and leave their wealth to others."

3. Proverbs 13:22; "A good man leaves an inheritance to his children's children, and the wealth of the sinner is stored up for the righteous."

C. Summary:

Accepting wealth from non-believers was a selective process because God always wants us to understand that it is his decision and provision that allows people to be wealthy. Therefore, Abraham would not accept the wealth of the Sodomites, but he would accept the bounty from the kings he fought to bring Lot back to Sodom and from the Pharaoh in Egypt. The Israelites accepted gifts from the Egyptians (notice this was used to build the tabernacle) but did not accept bounty from the Amorites.

Therefore, non-believers cannot view their gifts as blessings to believers, but gifts must be viewed by them as gifts and by believers as provisions from God. Israel accepted the gifts from Egypt because they were poor slaves. They used the homes etc., of the people in the promised land because Israel wandered in the wilderness for 40 years and did not have homes for their families.

II. The Church Taking Money Gathered from Non-Biblical Means

A. Money gained by non-biblical means can be beneficial for the poor:

1. Proverbs 28:8: "He who increases his wealth by interest and usury, gathers it for him who is gracious to the poor."

2. Exodus 22:25 "If you lend money to my people, to the poor among you, you are not to act as a creditor to him; you shall not charge him interest."

B. Money gained by non-biblical means can serve as a blessing to the righteous:

Ecclesiastes 2:26: "For to a person who is good in His sight He has given wisdom and knowledge and joy, while to the sinner He has given the task of gathering and collecting so that he may give to one who is good in God's sight. This too is vanity and striving after wind."

C. Money gained by non-biblical means for non-biblical reasons should not be accepted:

James 3:16-18: "For where jealousy and selfish ambition exist, there is disorder and every evil thing. But the wisdom from above is first pure, then peaceable, gentle, reasonable, full of mercy and good fruits, unwavering, without hypocrisy. And the seed whose fruit is righteousness is sown in peace by those who make peace."

III. The Application Of The Principles Discussed Above

A. The decision-making process for how the church responds to those who give whether they are saved or unsaved:

If a person calls and states that they have money to give to the church that was gathered from the lottery or gambling, the pastor will set a meeting with the elders to meet with this individual for the purpose of evaluating the motive of the gift. The following events will follow:

1. The elders will then meet after this meeting to decide what their recommendation will be to the deacons.

2. The deacons will meet to discuss the elder's recommendation. The deacons will respond with their recommendation to the elders.

3. The elders will meet and finalize their decision.

4. The person will then be contacted.

B. How does the church use this money?

1. The church can accept these gifts if the person providing them is only giving a gift. The money should be used to help the poor.

2. These gifts can come from foundations or organizations that do not consider themselves to be Christian.

   For example, suppose a car dealer donates a van to the church because our day-care is reaching some hurting people in the community. Should we refuse it?

3. The money will be used to minister to the poor who have legitimate needs through the outreach ministry.

C. How does the church respond to those who give or donate the money?

1. If it is an organization or foundation, we should write them an appropriate letter and report to them how the funds were used.

2. If it is an individual, we must write them a thank you letter and follow it up with a phone call.

3. The church must view this as a gift from God (II Chronicles 36:22; James 1:17).

   a) James 1:17: "Every good thing bestowed and every perfect gift is from above, coming down from the Father of lights, with whom there is no variation, or shifting shadow."

b) John 3:27: "John answered and said, "A man can receive nothing, unless it has been given him from heaven."

4. If a believer gave money to the church that was gained by non-biblical means (lottery etc.), the church must hold this believer accountable for his or her sin.

Conclusion

The concern about using money from non-believers or from believers who have gained it from means that violate God's Word is legitimate, but the money can be properly managed if the reason for giving or accepting the gift does not violate God's Word. We should use this money to impact the community, which would include helping the poor or those individuals who have legitimate needs.

10

Prophecy And The Church Today

Introduction

The purpose of this chapter is to define the role of prophecy in the New Testament Church. Is prophecy a revelation of the will of God as it relates to the future based on scripture for his redemptive purposes, or is it a spontaneous expression of what God is revealing to a believer for the sake of others? In the analyzing and outlining of this process we must define who is a prophet and what role they play in the Old Testament as compared to the New Testament. What is prophecy as compared to other forms of so called supernatural revelation, and how do believers who provide prophecy, function within the church?

I. Prophets And Prophetesses Of The Old And New Testament Spoke God's Will

Definition: A prophet is a believer that is sovereignly chosen by God to reveal to a people the will of God. This chosen believer of God functions under the total control of the Holy Spirit of God. They do not speak on their own initiative (Jeremiah

23:16; Ezekiel 13:1-7; Ephesians 3:1-7; II Peter 1:20-21). They only say what God has instructed them to say.

II. An Analysis Of The Word For Prophet In The Old And New Testament:

A. Old Testament:

1. The word in the Old Testament for prophet is *nabhi'*, used synonymously with 'seer,' which means "speaker." 'Seer' *hozeh* is an older term. This term related to people who can see divine revelations that others could not see. So this is a person who speaks divine revelation that only they can see.

2. The prophets of the Old Testament were believers who received a message directly from God (Numbers 22:8-9; I Kings 22: 14; Deuteronomy 18:18) as a result of visions, external voices or internal voices (Numbers 12:6; I Samuel 3:3-9; I Kings 13:18-22; Isaiah 1:1; Ezekiel 3:14). The hearing or seeing of these messages is something that no one else saw. It was a message that they must speak (Jeremiah 20:7,9). They were always conscious of the message they received. They never seemed to be in a trance. They clearly understood what was being told to them (Ezekiel 12:8). There is more authority given to these kinds of prophetic utterances than dreams or visions when someone may seem to be in a trance

(There is further discussion on this issue at point "5"). Several passages of scripture explain how this message came over them:

a) Fallen upon them (Ezekiel 11:5).

b) Laid hold of them (II Kings 3:15; Ezekiel 1: 3;3:14,22).

c) Came upon them (II Kings 2:15; I Chronicles 12:18; II Chronicles 24:20; Isaiah 42:1; 61:1).

d) Came in a cloud (Numbers 11:25).

e) Rest on them (Isaiah 11:2)

3. A prophetess in the Old Testament was a woman who like a male prophet revealed the will of God to the people (II Kings 22:14-20; Nehemiah 6:14: Exodus 15:20).

4. The exception to "2" is Moses who God spoke "mouth to mouth" (Numbers 12:7-8). God spoke to Moses openly before everyone.

5. A prophet receiving a dream was more focused on the interpretation of the dream and what it means for the future (Genesis 37:5-11; Daniel 2). Dreams sometimes came to people who were not prophets, not even believers, and it became the prophet's responsibility to interpret the person's dream (Nebuchadnezzar in Daniel 3, 4; Pharaoh, the cupbearer and the baker in Genesis 40, 41).

Jeremiah seems to imply that when a person uses dreams as a form of revelation from God; this should raise a 'red flag' for believers. *"I have heard what the prophets have said who prophesy falsely in my name, saying, 'I had a dream, I had a dream!' … who intend to make my people forget my name by their dreams, which they relate to one another, just as their fathers forgot my name because of Baal?* (Jeremiah 23:25,27). This is why some writers believe that dreams did not carry the same prophet authority as God directly speaking to his prophets. God seems to imply this in Jeremiah 23:29-32: *"Is not My word like fire?" declares the Lord, "and like a hammer which shatters a rock? Therefore behold, I am against the prophets," declares the Lord, "who steal my words from each other. Behold, I am against those who have prophesied false dreams," declares the Lord, "and related them, and led My people astray by their falsehoods and reckless boasting; yet I did not send them or command them, nor do they furnish this people the slightest benefit," declares the Lord.*

Each time dreams were recorded (Jacob, Joseph, Daniel, the wise men, and Peter); it seems that the dream was not as significant as God revealing his will to a prophet who then prophesied. *"Do not be hasty in word or impulsive in thought to bring up a matter in the presence of God. For God is in heaven and you are on earth; therefore let your words be few. For the dream comes through much effort, and the voice of a fool through many words"* (Ecclesiastes 5:2-3).

6. Because false prophets existed, the people were given these directions:

    a. "And you may say in your heart, 'How shall we know the word which the Lord has not spoke?' When a prophet speaks in the name of the Lord, if the thing does not come about or come true, that is the thing, which the Lord has not spoken. The prophet has spoke it presumptuously; you shall not be afraid of him" (Deuteronomy 18:21-22). The reason the people were not to be afraid of him is because God said the prophet would die.

    b. The age of the prophet did not matter. Jeremiah was a youth when he was called to prophesy (Jeremiah 1:6). The same is true for Samuel (I Samuel 3:1).

7. The message of the prophets took many forms:

    a. Divine judgment (II Kings 1:6).

    b. Divine salvation (II Kings 20:6).

    c. Judgment & salvation (Isaiah 65:7-8).

    d. Oracles of woe (Isaiah 5:8-23).

    e. Assurance (Jeremiah 30:10-11).

f. Encourage people to return to obeying God (Amos 4:4-5).

g. Sometimes the prophets were instructed to act out their message (Isaiah 20:2-4; Jeremiah 28:10).

h. Sometimes they predicted the future (Ezekiel 20:45-48).

8. Not every time a prophet spoke to reveal God's will about the future. God used credible called out prophets to reveal his will to the people so that they will have full knowledge of what God needed them to do. This is what Ezekiel, Jeremiah, Isaiah and most of the prophets of the Old Testament did.

B. The New Testament:

There are several words used in the New Testament for prophet, each having it's own meaning:

1. *Prophetes'* – which means "one who speaks forth." This word is derived from two words pro (before) and phemi (speak). This word corresponds with the Hebrew word *'nabhi'*. A person who speaks the will for God to people under the power of the Holy Spirit (Luke 1:67). As in the

Old Testament, the Holy Spirit empowered prophets to reveal his will. This caused them to speak with divine authority (reflect back to II, A, 2; page 100). **This is the most frequently used word in the New Testament. It is used a total of 144 times, 86 of these occurrences are found in the Gospels.**

2. '*Propheteuo*' – which means, "to proclaim a divine revelation" (Matthew 7:22), "to reveal prophetically what is hidden" (Matthew 26:68; Colossians 3:1-7), or "to foretell the future" (John 11:51). It is only used nine times in the Gospels.

3. '*Prophetis*' – which means "prophetess." This was was used in relation to women who prophesied for the Lord. (Anna in Luke 2:36-38; Elizabeth and Mary in Luke 1:41-45, 46-55; Philip's four virgin daughters, Acts 21:9; and in I Corinthians 11:5 where women assume the female role of prophesying).

4. When these three words are evaluated the office of the prophet or prophetess was not always used to address future events. It was primarily used to reveal or expose the will of God for believers.

C. The definition of prophets and prophetess as it relates to people in the Old and New Testament.

1. In Deuteronomy 18:14-22, God instructs us to

listen to his prophets and instructs how to recognize false prophets. The Lord does the same in the New Testament: "*But know this first of all, that no prophecy of Scripture is a matter of one's own interpretation, for* ***no*** *prophecy was ever made by an act of human will, but men moved by the Holy Spirit spoke from God*" (II Peter 1:20-21). Maybe this is why Paul viewed prophecy as edifying therefore it is better to prophesy than to speak in a tongue (I Corinthians 14:4-5). I Corinthians 14:5, 32-33 reads, "*Now I wish that you all spoke in tongues, but even more that you would prophesy; and greater is one who prophesies than one who speaks in tongues, unless he interprets, so that the church may receive edifying. For you can all prophesy one by one, so that all may learn and all may be exhorted?*"

How can these people learn? They can learn because, "*All Scripture is inspired by God and profitable for teaching, for reproof, for correction, for training in righteousness*" (II Timothy 3:16). This is why there is an accountability process; just like there was in the Old Testament, which was required for each message – "*But examine everything carefully; hold fast to that which is good*" (I Thessalonians 5:21). Unlike the Old Testament in the New Testament, prophecy is not tested based on whether or not it is fulfilled. Believers can now test through the power of the Holy Spirit whether or not prophecy is historically, grammatically and contextually true (Philippians 1:9-10; I John 2:20-21, 27; Acts 15:1-12; Acts 17:10-15).

Paul viewed prophecy as a revelation of revealed scripture, therefore, it will not return void. It is the power that all believers need to experience (I Corinthians 2:1-5). This is why anyone who prophesies, his or her prophecy should be examined carefully. *"Beloved, do not believe every spirit, but test the spirits to see whether they are from God, because many false prophets have gone out into the world"* (I John 4:1).Believers can test every spirit because every believer has *"an anointing from the Holy One, and you all know. I have not written to you because you do not know the truth, but because you do know it and because no lie is of the truth. And as for you, the anointing which you received from him abides in you, and you have no need for anyone to teach you; but as <u>the anointing teaches you about all things</u>, and is true and is not a lie, and just as it has taught you, you abide in him"* (I John 2:20-21, 27).

2. As explained earlier (this was done when we defined the meaning of prophecy, which is to reveal the will of God to his people), prophecy occurs when the prophet, who God speaks to directly, reveals the will of God for his people. These believers are then expected to obey the will of God as proclaimed by his prophet. If the proclamation proved to be wrong, the prophet was stoned to death (Deuteronomy 18:14-22). In the New Testament, the proclamation of God's will is ex posed as a result of the illumination of his Word (John 14:26; 16:13; I John 2:20-21, 27). The will of God for mankind is complete after Christ in spires the apostles to record the scriptures (John 17:20-23; II Timothy 3:14-17; Hebrews 1:1-4; II Peter 1:16-21). *"Grace and peace be multiplied to you in the knowledge of God and of Jesus our Lord; seeing that His divine power has granted to us everything pertaining to life and godliness, through the true knowledge of Him who called us by His own glory and excellence" II Peter 1:2-3).*

"And this I pray, that your love may abound still more and more in real knowledge and **<u>all discernment</u>***, so that you may approve the things that are excellent, in order to be sincere and blameless until the day of Christ" (Philippians 1:9-10).* *"For this reason also, since the day we heard of it, we have not ceased to pray for you and to ask that you may be filled with the knowledge* **<u>of His will in all spiritual wisdom and understanding</u>***, so that you may walk in a manner worthy of the Lord to* **<u>please Him in all respects</u>***, bearing fruit in every good work increasing in the knowledge of God" (Colossians 1:9-10).*

3. As the New Testament Church grows, the experience of the will of God is available to every believer. Every believer can know the perfect will of God. *"And do not be conformed to this world, but be transformed by the renewing of your mind, that you may prove what the will of God is, that which is good and acceptable and perfect"* (Romans 12:2). It is this renewed mind and the practicing of biblical principles that allow believers' senses to be trained to discern good and evil (Hebrews 5:14). This shows that the will of God is available as a result of the revelation of scripture for each believer. "*But when He, the Spirit of truth, comes, He will guide you into all the truth; for He will not speak on His own initiative; but* whatever He hears, He will speak; and He will disclose to you what is to come" (John 16:13).

4. Summary:

Prophecy of the Old and the New Testament was more focused on revealing the will of God to the people than future predictions. The predictions, when they did occur, were in the near (this allowed them to be tested) or the far future. When prophecy made predictions into the far future, many were Messianic and therefore tied into the New Testament eschatological picture. These Messianic prophecies are incorporated into the scripture of the New Testament.

"That which is given by the Spirit to the prophet can refer to the past and to the present as well as to the future. However, that which is revealed to the prophet finds its inner unity in this, that it all aims to establish the supremacy of Yahweh. Prophecy also views the detailed events in their relation to the divine plan, and the latter has for its purpose the absolute establishment of the supremacy of Yahweh in Israel and eventually in the entire earth." (C. VON ORELLI from International Standard Bible Encyclopedia, Electronic Database Copy

right (c) 1996 by Biblesoft.) Prophecy in the New Testament seems to be more directly attached to the scriptures. It is the correct explanation of the scriptures (II Timothy 2:15) that allows believers to be exposed to the will of God for their lives so that they can be equipped for every good work (II Timothy 4:11-16; II Timothy 3:16-17). This is why it is imperative for God's preacher to consistently preach sound doctrine (II Timothy 4:2), especially since the Church is the "pillar and foundation of truth" (I Timothy 3:15).

III. Prophecy As Compared To Other Forms Of So Called Supernatural Revelation

A. Introduction:

Now that we know who is a prophet and that prophecy occurs when this prophet reveals the will of God to people, the question that is before us is, "What is the difference between prophecy and other forms of supernatural revelation?" This is important because God did see other forms of supernatural revelation as being real, as is depicted in the case of Balaam (Numbers 22-24) as well as with Moses and the magicians in Egypt (Exodus 7-11). Another example is the witch at Endor (I Samuel 28:8-25) and the slave girl in Acts 16:16-21. During the tribulation period in Matthew 24:24, false prophets actually did perform signs and wonders. The fact that these signs and wonders are real causes God's elect to follow them.

"For false Christ and false prophets will arise and will show great signs and wonders, so as to mislead, if possible, even the elect" (Matthew 24:24). Paul warns us not to do the deeds of the flesh, which included sorcery and worship of idols (Galatians 5:20).

B. What is sorcery?

"Sorcery is the practice of the occult arts under the power of evil spirits, or demons, and has been common in all ages of the world's history." (From The New Unger's Bible Dictionary. Originally published by Moody Press of Chicago, Illinois. Copyright © 1988). Sorcery includes consulting mediums, witchcraft, interpreting omens, spiritism, calling up the dead, every form of magic, and the use of charms, e.g., rabbit foot.

C. The Word of God instructs us not to become involved in sorcery:

1. Leviticus 19:26 – *"You shall not eat anything with the blood, nor practice divination or soothsaying."*

2. Deuteronomy 18:9-15 – *"When you enter the land which the LORD your God gives you, you shall not learn to imitate the detestable things of those nations. There shall not be found among you anyone who makes his son or his daughter pass through the fire, one who uses divination, one who practices witchcraft, or one who interprets omens, or a sorcerer, or one who casts a spell, or a medium, or a spiritist, or one who calls up the dead. For whoever does these things is detestable to the LORD; and*

because of these detestable things the LORD your God will drive them out before you. You shall be blameless before the LORD your God. For those nations, which you shall dispossess, listen to those who practice witchcraft and to diviners, but as for you, the Lord your God has not allowed you to do so. The Lord your God will raise up for you a prophet like me from among you, from your countrymen, you shall listen to him."

3. All the Major Prophets spoke out against various forms of divination (Exodus 22:18; Isaiah 44:25; Jeremiah 27:9; 29:8; Ezekiel 13:9).

4. In the New Testament, the apostles address this issue when they confronted Simon the sorcerer in Acts 8:9-25, and Elymas in Acts 13:6-8.

5. The evil spirit attacked the seven sons of Sceva who practiced exorcists and beat them (Acts 19:13).

6. The Bible also denounces those who practice this form of demonic activity (Revelation 9:21; 18:23; 21:8; and 22:15).

D. There are several examples of how the Jews became involved in just about every form of sorcery:

1. Witchcraft and Mediums – Samuel and the witch of Endor (I Samuel 28:3,9) Isaiah addresses this

issue in 8:19 and 44:25. Jezebel's practice of witchcraft (I Kings 9:22).

2. Spiritism – Manasseh and his son Amon practiced spiritism (II Kings 21:6; II Chronicles 33:6, 21-25).
3. Enchantments or spells – The children of Israel practiced this form of sorcery (Isaiah 47:9,12; Psalm 58:4-5).

E. Summary:

Sorcery is depending on Satan to give people a word of direction for the situation they are experiencing. It is to no longer depend on God, but to believe in whatever the various forms of divination revealed. God punished them for their wickedness because he warned them not to be involved in the wickedness of the people in the promised land.

IV. Prophecy And The New Testament Church

A. Introduction:

The New Testament begins with God speaking to Zecharias (the husband of Elizabeth the father of John the Baptist) after four hundred years of silence. Even though Zecharias became dumb from his experience in the Holy of Holies as compared to Mary who hears from God (the second person for the angel to speak to), Elizabeth prophesies through the power of the Holy Spirit.

No one tied into the Old Testament prophets as John the Baptist did. John the Baptist so functioned in the power of the Holy Spirit impacting so many people (Matthew 14:5; 21:26; Luke 20:6) that he was asked on several occasions if he was 'the prophet' (John 1:21, 25; 7:52). No prophet, other than Christ, functioned as the Old Testament prophets did after John the Baptist.

He seems to have been the transitional prophet that tied the Old Testament to the New Testament as prophesied by Malachi (3:1). Jesus said; *"But why did you go out? To see a prophet? Yes, I say to you, and one who is more than a prophet. This is the one about whom it is written, 'Behold, I send my messenger before your face, who will prepare your way before you.' Truly, I say to you, among those born of women there has not arisen anyone greater than John the Baptist yet he who is least in the kingdom of heaven is greater than he"* (Matthew 11:9-11; Luke 7:26-28). John the Baptist followed the footsteps of the Old Testament prophets – having the impact on society the way they did. Everyone after Christ prophesied, but did not function as prophets in the same manner. The emphasis for the revealed Word of God seems to be tied more to the apostles (John 17:13-23) and the scripture they record (II Peter 1:20-21) than to prophets and the way they functioned in the Old Testament.

Even though prophets (Ephesians 2:20; 4:11) did share in the building of the Church's foundation (this is a reference to the Old Testament prophets as they spoke about Christ's birth, death, resurrection, etc.), the Church experienced the will of God for the people through pastor, teachers and the leaders of the churches (Ephesians 4:11-13; I Timothy 3:1-16; 4:11-16; 5:17-18; II Timothy

3:12-16). The Holy Spirit focused less on inspiring prophets more on the illumination of God's Word (John 16:13) and bringing God's Word back to believer's minds (John 14:26) for the renewal and transforming process (Romans 12:2).

B. An examination of the development of New Testament prophesy:

1. Elizabeth is the first person to prophesy. She was full of the Holy Spirit, who came upon her, and she prophesied (Luke 1:41).

2. Simeon, like the Old Testament prophets, experienced the Holy Spirit coming upon him and he prophesied (Luke 2:25-27).

3. Anna, like the Old Testament prophets, experienced the Holy Spirit coming upon her and she prophesied (Luke 2:36-38).

4. John the Baptist, as stated above, spoke like the Old Testament prophets.

5. We know that after Pentecost church leaders prophesied (Acts 7:55; 9:17; 11:24; 13:1).

6. There are others in the New Testament church that prophesied, e.g., Agabus (Acts 11:27-28), and the daughters of Philip (Acts 21:9).

7. In I Corinthians 11-14, an important transition occurred. When Paul speaks to the Corinthians in I Corinthians 11-14, he says that prophesying is a spiritual gift that is available to believers through the ministry of the Holy Spirit. The Holy Spirit sovereignly bestows this gift on believers. This was never seen to occur before; however, the Holy Spirit prophesied through a select group of individuals, never through the general population of a congregation.

   Paul however seems to place the inspiration under some accountable measures in an effort to maintain order in the church of Corinth. Everything must be done for the edification of the saints (I Corinthians 14:26-33). Paul concludes this section of scripture with the following: *"If anyone thinks he is a prophet or spiritual, let him recognize that the things which I write to you are the Lord's commandment. But if anyone does not recognize this, he is not recognized. Therefore, my brethren, desire earnestly to prophecy, and do not forbid to speak in tongues. But let all things be done properly and in an orderly manner"* (I Corinthians 14:37-40). Please note that the person who prophesies must not neglect "*the things which I write to you.*" Notice that they are *"the Lord's commandment."* John 14:15 says: *"If you love me you will keep my commandments."*

8. There is much discussion concerning I Corinthians

13:10 *"but when the perfect comes, the partial will be done away."* Some Bible teachers say that this represents the Word of God. Another based on I Corinthians 13:12: *"For now we see in a mirror dimly, but then face to face; now know in part, but then I shall know fully just as I also have been fully known."* *"Face to Face"* represents a time when we will stand before God, which will be after the rapture.

There are others who say that *"the perfect"* represents a time when the new heavens and the new earth are established. There is nothing in the text to support this view. Others state that this represents the perfect state of the Church at the coming of Christ. The later view fits the context of I Corinthians 13:8-13 better. Wycliff Commentary says: "That which is perfect cannot be a reference to the completion of the canon of Scripture; otherwise we now, living in the age of the completed canon, would see more clearly than Paul did (v. 9). Even the most self-satisfied and opinionated of theologians would hardly admit that. The coming of that which is perfect can only be a reference to the Lord's second coming. That event will mark the end of the exercise of prophecy, tongues, and knowledge. How then can one speak of these gifts as temporary? The following verse will answer the question." (from The Wycliffe Bible Commentary, Electronic Database. Copyright (c) 1962 by Moody Press.)

The following verse states that presently the gifts are childish. Verse 12, which begins with "now" means that Paul is speaking of the present. When this is tied to dimly (vs. 12), which associates with partial (vs. 8-9) what we now have compared to the perfect is childish (vs. 11). Now when we compare our present situation to the full revelation at the second coming of Christ, we will not need these gifts to understand the kingdom of God. We will have full (perfect, complete) exposure to what God is saying to us and this is why we do not need prophesy at the coming of Christ. This means at the second coming of Christ; the perfect has come. There will be no need for prophecy. Therefore, before the second coming of Christ, there is still a need for prophecy.

9. When Paul outlines to Timothy the process for setting the church in order, Paul instructed Timothy to be on guard against false teaching, to organize worship, to define the role of women in the church, and the role and function of elders and deacons. Then he told Timothy that the church is now set in order. This not only set the church in order, it established the church to be *"the pillar and foundation of truth"* (I Timothy 3:15-16). Timothy as a result must now focus *"on the words of the faith,"* and *"sound doctrine,"* exposed through revealed scripture (I Timothy 4:6, 13). Timothy is told to *"pay attention to his teaching,"* and it is these things he must prescribe (I Timothy 4:16).

These things lead to edification (I Timothy 4:16). His teaching must come from the scriptures, which he must study (II Timothy 2:15), so that *"the man of God may be adequate, equipped for* **every** *good work"* (II Timothy 3:17). The emphasis is on scripture not on a need for spontaneous revelation but on the revealed word of God.

10. By spontaneous revelation, we mean instances when a person claims to hear God speaking to them, then they utter what they believe came from God. This is exactly what Ecclesiastes addresses when Solomon says: *"Do not be hasty in word or impulsive in thought to bring up a matter in the presence of God. For God is in heaven and you are on the earth; therefore let your words be few. For the dream comes through much effort, and the voice of a fool through many words"* (Ecclesiastes 5:2).

11. The latter churches (as found in I, II Timothy and Titus; even the churches in Revelation that neglected the Word of God), as compared to the early churches in the book of Acts, and I Corinthians, seem to emphasize the revealed Word of God, rather than a reliance on spontaneous prophetic utterances. Peter states in I Peter 1:22-25; *"Since you have in obedience to the truth purified your souls for a sincere love of the brethren, fervently love one another from the heart, for you have been born again not of seed which is perishable, but imperishable, that is, through the living and enduring word of God. For,*

'ALL FLESH IS LIKE GRASS, AND ALL ITS GLORY LIKE THE FLOWER OF GRASS. THE GRASS WITHERS, AND THE FLOWER FALLS OFF, BUT THE WORD OF THE LORD ENDURES FOREVER.' And this is the word which was preached to you." There is a greater reliance on the Scriptures than on a spontaneous utterance. The apostle John writes; *"Beloved, I am not writing a new commandment to you, but an old commandment which you have had from the beginning; the old commandment is the word which you have heard. On the other hand, I am writing a new commandment to you, which is true in him and in you, because the darkness is passing away and the true Light is already shining"* (I John 2:7-8).

John then instructs them to rely on the Holy Spirit to reveal the truth (this is because the Church is the pillar and foundation of truth. This is a foundation that Christ laid that no one must change – I Corinthians 3:10), and not to listen to false teachers that are seeking to influence them (I John 2:20-21, 25-27). It is the Word of God that produces faith (Romans 10:17) and it is faith that pleases God (Hebrews 11:6). The apostles wrote with authority. They expected the New Testament saints to trust their words (I John 1:1-4; 2:7-8; I Peter 1:22-25; II Timothy 3:16-17).

They became the prophets of the New Testament influencing believers everywhere to follow their teachings. This is exactly what Christ prayed for: *"And for their sakes I sanctify myself, that they themselves also may be sanctified in truth. I do not ask in behalf of these alone, but for those also* ***who believe in me through their Word"*** (John 17:19-20). This is the same thing we read in Acts 2:42: *"And* ***they were continually devoting themselves to the apostles' teaching*** *and to fellowship, to the breaking of bread and to prayer."* Hebrews 1:1-13 states, *"God, after He spoke long ago to the fathers in the prophets in many portions and in many ways, in these last days has spoken to us in His Son, whom He appointed heir of all things, through whom also He made the world."*

12. Many passages of scripture emphasize the need for believers to place trust and commitment to their daily walk in the revealed Word of God. Romans 12:2: *"And do not be conformed to this world, but be transformed by the renewing of your mind, that you may prove what is the will of God is, that which is good and acceptable and perfect."* Romans 10:17: *"So faith comes from hearing,and hearing by the word of Christ."* Philippians 1:9-10: *"And this I pray, that your love may abound still more and more in real knowledge and all discernment so that you may approve the things that are excellent, in order to be sincere and blameless until the day of Christ."* Colossians 1:9-10: *"For this reason also, since the day we heard of it, we have not ceased to pray for you and ask that you may be filled with the knowledge of His will in all spiritual wisdom and understanding, so that you may walk in a manner worthy of the Lord,* ***to please Him in all respects, bearing***

fruit in every good work *and increasing in the knowledge of God."*
II Timothy 3:16-17: *"All Scripture is inspired by God and profitable for teaching, for reproof, for correction, for training in righteousness; that the man of God may be adequate, equipped for every good work."* Hebrews 5:13-14: *"For everyone who partakes only of milk is not accustomed to the word of righteousness for he is a babe. But solid food is for the mature, who because of practice have their senses trained to discern good and evil."* These scriptures and others teach believers to rely on the revealed Word of God as a means of gaining faith (Romans 10:17), learning the good, acceptable and perfect will of God, (Romans 12:2), being able to develop a spirit of discernment for good decision making (Philippians 1:9-11), growing in wisdom and understanding (Colossians 1:9-10) as well as to mature as a believer (Hebrews 5:14). By applying these scriptures, a believer can reach full maturity in Christ. As a result of the revealed scripture a believer would have "*everything pertaining to life and godliness, through the true knowledge of him who called us by his own glory and excellence*" (II Peter 1:3).

13. This section clearly demonstrates that believers must focus more on the revealed Word of God rather than spontaneous revelation.

C. The importance of the Apostles as it relates to scripture:

1. When Christ came, he said that he was only saying what the Father instructed Him to say (John 14:10). Christ functioned as the prophet revealing the will of God for the people. He told them of the past, the present and the future (John 12:44-50).

2. Christ transfered this responsibility to the apostles (John 17:13-23) because he told them that he would only speak to the people in parables, because it is the apostles who would expose to the people the will of God (Matthew 13:11-17). Make note of very significant statements in John 17:13-17: *"I have given them thy word (the word He spoke for God; John 12:44-50); and the world has hated them because they are not of the world, even as I am not of the world." (vs. 14) "Sanctify them in the truth; Thy word is the truth." (vs. 17) For their sakes I sanctify myself, that they themselves also may be sanctified in truth. I do not ask in behalf of these alone, but for those also who believe in Me through their word" (vs. 19-20).* The Word of God is now transferred to us through the writings of the apostles who serve as the foundation of the Church, which is Christ (I Corinthians 3:10-11; Ephesians 2:20).

3. Notice in Hebrews 1:1-2, we read the following: *"God, after He spoke long ago to the fathers in the prophets in many portions and in many ways, in these last days has spoken to us in His Son, whom He appointed heir of all things, through whom also He made the world."*

a. In the Old Testament God used "*prophets in many portions and many ways*;" major prophets and minor prophets the great prophet Moses and the small prophet Obadiah.

b. In the New Testament times, Christ has provided his Word, which is from God, through the apostles (John 17:13-19). This is why the apostles play a significant part in laying the foundation for the New Testament Church (Ephesians 2:20).

D. Summary:

As the church grew older and the Word of God was recorded, the church relied more on the revealed scripture than on prophetic utterances. It is the renewing of the mind attached to these recorded scriptures that leads to a transformed life, which reveals the perfect will of God [(Romans 12:2). This is what prophets (note page 104) did for God]. The Holy Spirit who is Christ's helper works in believers to illuminate the Word of God (John 14:26; I John 2:20-21, 27).

This is why anyone in a congregation can prophesy in an orderly manner (I Corinthians 14). Since all scripture is inspired and equips the man of God for every good work, the need for spontaneous utterances of God's word has changed to a greater emphasis on teaching and living according to scripture (II Peter 1:20-21). It is inspiration given to the apostles (II Timothy 3:16) that will reveal the mysteries of God's will, the past, present and future

(Revelation).

Conclusion

Is prophecy a revelation of scripture or is it a spontaneous expression of what God is revealing to a believer for the sake of others? The progressive revelation of God's Word, as it was with Moses, relies more on the written Word of God than it does on the oracles of prophets. When Moses first spoke, the emphasis of his message was to prophesy what the will of God was for the people. Then God led Moses to record scripture. Until the time of Eli, the people relied heavily on the writings of Moses.

Hilkiah discovered these writings during the reign of Josiah and it is these writings that led to reform in Judea (II Chronicles 34:8-33). After the kings, and the judges, God spoke to the people using prophets (in many portions and many ways Hebrews 1:1) in an effort to turn the people back to God by obeying the Word of God as written in Genesis through Deuteronomy. For 400 years, there was a period of silence when God did not speak to or through anyone. Then God continued where he left off by speaking through John the Baptist (Malachi 4:5; Matthew 11:9-17), then through Jesus Christ, many others in the early beginnings of the New Testament Church and finally through the apostles who recorded God's Word. All New Testament believers, like those during the time of Moses, must now rely on the recorded scripture of God's Word.

God has not stopped speaking through his Son (Hebrews 1:1-3). He continually speaks to us through the power of the Holy Spirit (John 14:16-31) to explain the meaning of scripture, as it relates to the future, and to prophecy. Since we have explained that prophecy is the revealed Word of God (scripture) and we must rely and trust in it, we must not depend on spontaneous expressions that claim to be the revealed will of God. To God be the glory!

11

The Role Of Women In The Local Church

Introduction

The role of women in the local church has created tremendous struggles and divisions among believers over the past 20 years. The purpose of writing on this subject is not to intensify the struggle for this would only serve to cause more harm than benefit to the body of Christ. But rather, my hope is that at the end of this study; women would have a clearer unadulterated biblical understanding of their equality with men and their God given function in and for the body of Christ and the same for men that they would understand women's equality with men biblically, and the man's God given role in and for the body the Christ.

This dilemma has been reinforced as a result of women being involved in abusive relationships, increased divorces, increased single-parent homes, apathetic male leadership in the home and the church, and the imbalance of women in church as compared to men. This has caused women to be forced into leadership roles at home and in the church.

This issue however must not be addressed philosophically because this would lead to relativism. Relativism occurs when the issue is logically evaluated and the conclusions are then sought after for biblical support, so that the intent of scripture becomes whatever it needs to be for any individual. This is why the focus of this chapter will be to evaluate every passage within its context through a grammatical-historical interpretation of the text. This means that the language, of the particular passage, will be evaluated within its normal meaning, and interpreted within its historical context. This will be done carefully, since the writer of any passage had only one meaning in mind when he wrote it. There could be many applications, but only one interpretation.

Many persons may however hold these interpretations suspect because they will retain the view that the New Testament culture was operating in a completely different culture, or that the N.T. culture by its very nature would have given support for a limited view. This interpretation is what I call "a hide and seek" interpretation of scripture. Hide from those passages that do not support a particular view and seek those that will. Scripture must be viewed objectively and authoritatively. We must not allow our traditions or sociological premises to cloud the true interpretation of scripture.

Bear in mind that Jesus, the Word of God living in flesh, did not allow culture to influence his Father's scriptural intent when he healed on the Sabbath (Mark 1:21-27), cleansed the temple (John 2:14-17), spoke to a Samaritan woman (John 4:7-9), and ate with tax collectors and sinners (Mark 7:1-23). God's biblical intent is pure and focused, and healthy for both men and women, whom he created. It's our biased views that have contributed to the confusion, and to inaccurate interpretation of scripture.

Deborah's Role As A Judge And How This Relates To The Church

Many individuals have used Deborah to establish that women can be pastors, so let us examine this supposition expositionally. Two major areas attached to many sub-points must be deduced. First, we'll consider Deborah's position as judge and prophetess, and secondly her function as a military leader. In order to do this, we must define who is a judge as compared to a pastor in terms of position and function. We must also examine the role of a prophetess as compared to a pastor's role as a teacher, and Deborah's leadership for Israel as compared to leadership in the church.

However, before we begin this process, it is important to remember that the book of Judges records a period in Israel's history where there was little order because the Israelites for the most part had turned their backs on God. It was a time of chaos; "everyone did as he saw fit" (Judges 21:25 NIV). It is for this very reason that Paul seeks to establish order in the New Testament Church (I Corinthians 14:40; I Timothy 3:15).

The word "pastor" or "shepherd," is representative of the meaning of the word "elder." The appointment of elders in the Old Testament was restricted to men who were respected because of their spirituality and leadership: "select capable men from all the people - men who fear God, trustworthy men who hate dishonest gain ... ." (Take note to how many times he mentions men; Exodus 18:21; Deuteronomy 1:13). This is repeated in the New Testament (I Timothy 3:1-5; II Timothy 2:2) "Entrust to reliable men who will also be qualified to teach".

Customarily, the elders took their positions at the city gates, but Deborah sat "under the palm tree of Deborah between Ramah and Bethel in the hill country of Ephraim" (Judges 4:5), clearly demonstrating her understanding of her role. The elders and the priests provided spiritual insight for the people of Israel; whereas, a judge judged the civil matters. Because the people of Israel were doing evil in God's eyes (Judges 4:1), there were probably more civil matters to judge than there was a need for spiritual insight (after all they were not pursuing God and his law). This is why it was not surprising that she became Israel's leader in another civil matter, which was to release Israel from Jabin's cruel oppression (Judges 4:3, 5). Deborah however, clearly understood her role obeyed God, and sent for Barak.

Deborah is the only female judge in the book of Judges, and in her case there is no record that God intervened and directly called her as he did in every other instance. The people came to her, but God told her to get Barak (Judges 4:6) whose response demonstrates why God allowed Deborah to lead. This could also be the reason Barak is mentioned in Hebrews (11:32). Please do not misunderstand me. I am not insinuating that God thinks less of women. God certainly does not; he views us as joint heirs (I Peter 3:7).

I am simply examining scripture, and it is clear that Deborah understood and honored God's order and process. A prophet/prophetess is someone who is called by God (Jeremiah 1:4-8), to speak only what God instructs, and to interpret God's will for man (Exodus 7:1-2; 4:4-16; Deuteronomy 18:14-22). The messages were mostly but not always focused on revealing God's will for the Jews during Israel's turbulent history or the New Testament Church.

Their messages were held as authoritative. If found to be false, they were stoned to death (Deuteronomy 13:1-5; 18:20-22). The people received directions and instructions based on the Pentateuch (Leviticus 10:11; Deuteronomy 21:5; Malachi 2:6-7) and the Mosaic laws, from priest, elders and judges, in that specific order. There were times when priest, elders, judges, and kings prophesied (David in the Psalms), but they were not considered totally as prophets. They just made a prophetic utterance, which is why they were not part of the school of prophets. So there is a clear distinction based on primary function among priests, elders, judges (Deuteronomy 1:15-16), and prophets/prophetesses (Exodus 7:1-2).

Even though women were prophetesses, they were not priests or elders who were the primary leaders in Israel. In the New Testament, you will find the same thing occurring (I Timothy 3:1-2; II Timothy 2:2). Even though women were allowed to prophesy, they were told to respect the leadership of the church (I Corinthians 11:3-6). Deborah clearly understood these distinctions. There was also an understanding in the Old Testament that one day God will send pastors who will be shepherds (Jeremiah 3:15) not prophets/prophetesses. This process is adapted by Paul in Ephesians 4:11 "...gave some to be apostles, ...prophets, ...evangelists, ...pastors and teachers."

However, the prophets'/prophetesses' role in the Old Testament were distinct and significant, their role in the New Testament did not have the same authority or significance because Christ used a different method to reveal his hidden truth, namely the apostles (Ephesians 1:9; 3:6). Paul told the church to sort and sift through all prophetic utterances: "Do not despise prophesying, but test everything; hold fast what is good" (I

Thessolonians 5:20-21; I Corinthians 14:29-33a), meaning everything Paul told them (II Timothy 2:2). So it is the apostles who now have the authority to reveal God's truth as expressed through Jesus Christ (Hebrews 1:2; Ephesians 2:20). It is the pastors' function who are the elders in the New Testament; like it was for the high priests and elders to teach it to believers, so that each Christian would apply these principles to their daily lives. The roles of Deborah or the prophetess found in Acts 2:17; 21:9 were different than that of a pastor.

A Biblical Overview of I Timothy 2:11-14

In the Old Testament (Genesis 1:27) and the New Testament, it is obvious that God views women and men as equal. I Peter 3:7 states that Christian women and men are joint heirs, and I Corinthians 11:11-12 supports this view as well as Galatians 3:28. It is also plain that the Bible states that men and women are given spiritual gifts for the equipping of the saints (I Corinthians 12:7-11; 12:12-26; I Peter 4:10; Ephesians 4:13-16). The question that we must now address is why when it is a worship service, would Paul state that women should "learn in quietness and full submission. I do not permit a woman to teach or to have authority over a man" (I Timothy 2:11-14; I Corinthians 14:34-35).

This is the same writer who seems to allow women to pray and prophesy during worship (I Corinthians 11:5,13). The question is how do we explain this concept, and does the apostle Paul contradict himself? Many individuals have written books on this issue. It would be impossible to answer this question in one chapter, however a summary would be in order.

Paul left Timothy to pastor the church at Ephesus. During Paul's absence, the church became unsettled due to false teachers who had infiltrated the church. These false teachers had created arguments concerning doctrines associated with asceticism, which included women and their roles in marriage, the distinct roles for men and women in the church, and it is believed by many writers that many of the women in the church became involved in promoting this doctrine (I Timothy 2:11-15; 4:3-8). This is very similar to what occurs in I Corinthians. It is in the midst of this controversy that Paul writes to a young pastor, Timothy.

Paul's focus is to set things back in order (I Timothy 3:15), so that the church in Ephesus, like the Corinthian church, would function decently and in God's order (I Corinthians 14:40). Order for the sake of Godly function is the issue here not equality. Many people claim that Paul was influenced by his culture. This does not hold water because in Paul's culture women were not put in positions where they would learn, yet Paul is encouraging them to position themselves to learn. Women were not allowed to say anything when men gathered to teach etc., but it is Paul who allows them to pray and prophesy.

It is Paul who compliments many women serving in the ministry in Acts and Romans. Paul was more of a radical than a conformist. Just ask brother Peter when he visited Antioch in Galatians 2:11-21. Some may debate that Paul did not want the women to teach because women were not allowed to teach men during this period (asceticism was being promoted by some women in the church), and he did not want the church to have a poor reputation in Ephesus. The church's reputation is important to Paul, but Paul was not seeking to resolve this for that reason. He addresses this issue so that Christ will be glorified (I Timothy 1:16; 2:14-15; Ephesians 1:12).

If all scripture is inspired by God and all of it is, then Paul led by the Holy Spirit wrote I Timothy 2:11-14 in obedience to God sensitive to cultural dynamics but not controlled by it. Teaching, with the primary reference being in the church, represented a careful transmission of the teachings of Jesus Christ (Matthew 28:20; I Timothy 1:13), and the authoritative proclamation of God's will for believers (I Timothy 4:11; II Timothy 2:2; Acts 2:42; Romans 12:7). This activity was clearly restricted to those who were provided the gift of teaching, whether men or women (I Corinthians 12:28-30; Ephesians 4:11), and these individuals as stated in James 3:1 as well as Matthew 5:19; 18:5-6 will be judged more strictly. This is why since women are equal to men and can be given the gift of teaching, many women can sometimes teach even more effectively than some men. The issue is not whether or not women can teach, but can they teach when men are present?

God's Word, by its very nature, is authoritative (John 14:15; this word "command" in Timothy means to "have authority over" or "dominate" in the naturally sense of "having dominion over"). Anyone teaching it would be exercising this authority when teaching especially since teaching not only involved instruction and observation, but also accountability; "to him that knoweth what to do and does not do it, to him it is sin." God's Word is perfect, and mankind is sinful. Teaching the perfect Word of God to sinful people means that the person teaching will be authoritatively correcting those who are listening. This is why we find passages such as II Timothy 3:16 "... useful for teaching, rebuking, correcting and training in righteousness ...," as well as II Timothy 4:2, "Preach the word; be prepared in season and out of season; correct, rebuke and encourage ... ."

This is why Paul encourages Timothy to entrust this to reliable men in II Timothy 2:2 and it was a continuation from the home to the church (II Timothy 3:3-4). The home illustrated how the church functioned (Ephesians 5:32), and the church was to support and strengthen the function of the home. Just imagine how confusing this would be for a child or anyone else. In the home, the father is told to teach (Genesis 18:18-19; Ephesians 5:25-27), and have authority over his wife (I Corinthians 11:3; Ephesians 5:22-23), but when the child attends church, the mother is teaching the father, telling him how to live authoritatively. But God told us to function decently and in order (I Corinthians 11:3; 14:40). This is one of the reasons Paul shifted the discussion in this passage (II Timothy 2:11-14) to Adam and Eve and told Timothy not to allow the women "to teach or to have authority over a man..."

This chapter is in no way seeking to degrade or insult women in ministry. My mother taught all eight of her children at 6:30 every morning and did a great job. Four of us are in full-time ministry and everyone except one brother who is saved, is serving God in some way. Timothy's mother and grandmother also did a great job a job, which Paul views as significant. I am seeking to provide a biblical expositional overview in an effort to furnish clarity to an issue that is dividing our community and disturbing many services in our churches.

To Paul (yes, we are still discussing I Timothy 2:11-14), this issue of whether women should teach men was already addressed in Genesis an account which most of us would view as only relative to the home, and the origin of sin. In the writing of Ephesians, Paul instructs during his discussion on marriage that the focus of his discourse was about the church (Ephesians 5:22-33). Paul also states in Timothy that a man must have his home in order before he is qualified to be a leader and teacher in the church (I Timothy 3:4-5). So God's creation order did not just set the foundation for how a man and woman should function in marriage.

It also established the process for how they should function in the church. In I Timothy 2:14, Paul is stating that Eve reversed the order God set when by the very manner in which she was born, and by the very nature of her name. God established his order not after the fall, but before the fall. When she told Adam what to do, and demonstrated a sense of independence by eating the fruit before giving it to him, she created chaos rather than worship to God. Therefore what occurred in Genesis provided Paul the context for the role of women in the church. So to legitimize women teaching men, we would have to reverse the theological base from which God develops everything. If you reverse the order who is going to outline the process (write another Bible), and maintain it?

However, Paul did not exit this discussion without providing an encouraging perspective for the women in church. Paul states in verse 15, "But women shall be preserved (saved, KJ) through the bearing of children if they continue in faith and love and sanctity with self-restraint." I know that what I have just stated may anger some feminists, but the emphasis here is not on having babies. It is what results. The Martin Luther Kings, Kay Jameses, and Timothys blessed the Christian community when raised in a godly manner. When these women get to heaven, God will preserve for them a tremendous blessing that they would enjoy for eternity. In other words, Paul is stating that the order God has created has tremendous benefit for the congregation and women if women function (self-restraint) relevant to God's plan.

Equality and Role Distinctions in the Church

Genesis 1:26-27; 5:1-2; Galatians 3:28

Many individuals state that men and women were created equal but the fall caused God to put the male over the female, which was a part of God's punishment. However, since we are now living under grace and those who accept Christ are redeemed, women are released from male headship because it was a part of God's punishment. This, they would state, affects how males and females function in the church, thus allowing women to preach or teach whether or not there are any men present. We will begin our discussion by examining expositionally Genesis 1:26-27; 5:1-2 and continue with Galatians 3:28. Conclusions from this discussion will help us to define biblical equality and how God's authoritative view affects the distinctive roles of men and women in the local church.

It is obvious that God viewed men and women as equal as outlined in Genesis 1:26-27 and Genesis 5:2. The word image or likeness means to mirror God in his spirituality, not physical form, since God is spirit (II Corinthians 2:10-11). As a result, men and women can equally have God's Spirit. This is why a woman can grow to spiritual maturity, and have spiritual gifts like any man. The biblical question however is not spiritual equality for God, Christ and the Holy Spirit are equal. It is role distinction for the purpose of carrying out God's plan (Ephesians 1:11). For mankind was made in God's image to demonstrate God's glory through good works as Paul states in Ephesians 2:10. Paul repeats this in I Corinthians 10:31; Colossians 3:17.

God had Adam name all the animals not just to establish

his dominion but also to recognize his need. All the animals appeared in pairs, but Adam was single, "But for Adam no suitable helper was found." When Adam recognized his need, as he was busy doing God's will, God supplied a suitable helper. In order for someone to be a suitable helper they need to have the same capacity that the person they are helping has to be helpful. To make sure that the help was suitable (God took Eve out of Adam's side, not foot) God took it upon himself to create Eve. Eve had the same capacity, but Adam recognized that she was certainly different (Genesis 2:23). Adam should be able to clearly recognize the difference since he had spent the day naming animals based on their differences. So it was not a matter of equality; it was a difference in roles, and function within God's plan.

Also keep in mind that it was Adam who named Eve "woman," not God. Because in God's creation process, he outlines his order and establishes man's headship only so that man, with a suitable helper in the woman, will carry out God's plan, purpose and will. None of the above occurred after the fall. It all took place before the fall so it was not punishment. It was and is God's plan. Many individuals have stated since Galatians 3:27-28 says that men and women are equal in Christ, what difference does it make if women preach when men are present?

As stated above, equality between men and women has never been an issue biblically. Genesis 1:26 supports equality, "Let us make man (meaning mankind) in our image, in our likeness ... ." So God created man in his own image ... And God blessed them ... ." However even though God created men and women with the same capacity to experience and exhibit God, God patterned how that will work itself out by making mankind male and female, so that each gender functions differently both naturally and spiritually. Naturally in that females have the capacity to have children; whereas, men do not. Therefore men and women are physically different. They are spiritually different not in terms of their capacity to experience the work of God in their lives, "For we are his workmanship created in Christ Jesus to do good works, which God had before ordained that we should walk in them" (Ephesians 2:10) but in their responsibility to God, and the body of Christ represented by believers, the Church.

Paul told men in Ephesus of their responsibility to their wives, "cleansing her by the washing with water through the word … ." (Ephesians 5:26). This was carried over to the church (I Timothy 3:4-5). Paul also told the wives to ask their husbands questions after church about the Word of God (I Corinthians 14:35). There are differences in function, even though there is true equality. Galatians 3:27-28 is the biblical hallmark for equality, but the discussion has nothing to do with biblical responsibility and function.

The focus of the passage was on informing the Jews, who were still practicing the ceremonial law, and requiring the Gentiles to do the same and become circumcised that all men are saved by grace – not the law. This is the very same discussion that Paul had in Romans 3-5. Paul was seeking to inform them that there is no difference between Jews, Gentiles, and bond or free because it is faith in Jesus Christ that saves, not being of Abraham or by obeying the law. So equality between men and women is not an issue in Galatians. The Bible supports women as being equal with men before and after the fall (I Peter 3:7), but there is a distinction in function both naturally and spiritually. This distinction is focused on manifesting God's glory and illustrating the Church (Ephesians 5:27,32).

When these differences create divisions and conflict, both the manifestation and the illustration are hampered and men or women gets the praise not God. This is why I believe that surveys show that people are beginning to lose faith in the church. They want the truth, but they fail to see a complete illustration of it.

Conclusion

This issue will continue to be debated until Jesus comes back. I do pray however that leaders will examine the subject comprehensively, and biblically. (A good book that can be a guide to your study is "Recovering Biblical Manhood & Womanhood," by John Piper and Wayne Grutten). This subject unfortunately is discussed too many times, more philosophically then biblically. Many individuals seek to project ideas they believe "make sense" rather than what is biblically truth. We must remember that each author in the Bible was only seeking to communicate one concept not a multiplicity of concepts.

We must be true to the author's intent not make scripture fit our conclusions that "make sense." "For the foolishness of God is wiser than man's wisdom, and the weakness of God is stronger than man's strength" (I Corinthians 1:25). This issue, as I have stated above is not one of equality. Rather can women teach or preach when men are present or be pastors? It is biblically incorrect to state that the Bible supports women preaching and teaching when men are present.

There is no way that it can be biblically supported that women can pastor. This is explicitly outlined in scripture. Somehow individuals have stretched this to imply that women do not have anything to do in the church. This is not true. Some churches, I know have 115 ministries that women can serve in. **Some examples are women, such as Phoebe who plays a significant role in the church at Cenchrea and women who assisted the deacons with their ministry in the church of Ephesus (Romans 16:1-3; I Timothy 3:11).** Titus 2:3-5 instructs the older women to teach the younger women. Women can sing and direct the music in the church; women can be allowed to provide instruction to a man, in the company of their husbands (Acts 18:26). Women can direct a variety of ministries in the church.

To summarize, as explained above, this issue has nothing to do with equality. It has nothing to with women and their spiritual gifts. The prophetesses' or prophets' role, functionally within the local church, were not the same as a pastor/teacher. Deborah's ministry based on proper biblical analysis cannot be used as an example for women being preachers or pastors. The New Testament consistently portrays women being actively involved in ministry whether it is helping Christ, Paul or the church, but scripture does not explicitly or consistently support women preaching, pastoring or teaching men in the local congregations.

In a community, where morals and values are no longer upheld as the standard, but where confusion, frustration and devastation is the norm, we need to uphold the Word of God as the standard in the one place that meets weekly to teach morals and values, the church. With the breakdown of the family, we need to see men taking their roles seriously, leading and guiding their homes from the Word of God, as a result of their exemplary lives that have been impacted by the Word. If this does not occur, history as seen in the book of Judges will repeat itself.

12

Women And Head Covering

Introduction

The purpose for examining this issue is to explain whether the wearing of head covering, when a woman is teaching with men present, is relevant for the Church today. I Corinthians 11:3-16 is the passage we will examine to provide an explanation for this issue. Also by explaining this issue, the role of women in the church, will become more defined for the effective development of the church. This chapter can serve as "Part II" for the position paper on "The Role of Women in the local Church."

I. Understanding The Problem In I Corinthians 11:3-16

Historical Background:

Women in the Jewish community functioned under a strict set of laws. In the Jewish community, women were not allowed to pray in synagogues, and the community played down women who called themselves prophetesses. Women were not allowed to teach or admonish others (prophesying 13:9; 14:1,3,24,31,39) in worship (I Corinthians 14:34; I Timothy 2:11-15). When Paul planted churches, many of the people felt liberated from these laws. (Paul taught that "you were saved by grace" not by obeying the law; Romans 4; 1 Corinthians 6:12; 10:23-25).

Because the church was a mixture of Jews and Gentiles, this new found freedom created problems. Some of the Gentiles' customs allowed women not to wear a head covering, but these women were not allowed to wear their hair loose. Wearing loose hair was something the upper-class women loved to do. The Gentiles viewed a loose-haired woman as provoking lust in a man (probably the same way many people view a bikini bathing suit). So, women had to braid their hair. The Jews viewed women who did not have a head covering whether their hair was worn loose or not as women who were seeking to attract a man. If a woman cut off her hair, she was considered a prostitute. So, with both Jews and Gentiles in the church women's identities were determined not just by what they wore or how they conducted themselves but also by how they cared for their hair.

The differences in the cultures plus the new found freedom of many of the Jews (some of the Jews still held to the old way) and Gentiles created problems in the church. Women who once respected the man's presence in worship and did not say anything, were now speaking out loud during the worship service. Women who once wore head coverings were no longing wearing head coverings. This, along with speaking in strange tongues and people taking each other to court, created a chaotic situation in the church. The complexity of this situation caused Paul to write this book. It also created a need for the proper order of worship to be outlined.

II. Outline of the Problem Addressed in I Corinthians 11:3-16:

A. Is Paul telling the women to wear a head covering when they are praying or prophesying as a sign of submission to the headship of man?

B. Is head covering the same as long hair?

C. Is head covering something of concern only for Paul's culture and not ours?

III. An Analysis of I Corinthians 11:3-16

A. Introduction:

Paul in this section of I Corinthians is seeking to explain how the believers in the church should function in public worship as it relates to women in the church (11:3-16), the Lord's Supper (11:17-34), and spiritual gifts (12:1-14:40). This issue of the head covering examines primarily, how women function in public worship.

B. An Analysis of the Passage:

1. Head Covering:

It is obvious that based on verses 6-7, and the implied reference in verse 5 and 13 that Paul is telling women that they should wear a head covering when they prophesy in worship service.The Greek word for cover (*katakalypto*) represented some kind of covering or veil. In the Old Testament (LXX version) it is used in Isaiah 6:2 when the angels covered their faces, and Genesis 38:15 when Tamar covered her face. In verse 15, it seems as if Paul is rejecting his call for a covering or veil.

He seems to state that women's long hair served as their covering, so a covering or veil was not necessary. Paul was not contradicting himself. Rather, he was saying that women's long hair was given to them "AS" (The Greek word *avti* could mean "as," "for" or "instead of;" "as" is used in the the New International Version Bible) a covering. This means that women's long hair was an indication that they needed a covering (review the background on page 143-144 to understand the significance of this). The interpretation of the Greek word *avti* "as" better relates to the context of the passage. Paul not only stated that women needed a covering but he also compared this with a man not wearing a covering while praying or prophesying (vs. 7).

Paul also states, in this verse, that a man does not wear a head covering because he is the image of God (this is a reference back to verse 3). Woman, however, is the glory of the man, and her hair serves as her glory (vs. 15). Therefore, the issue of head covering was not just related to women prohesying but also to maintaining the order that Paul outlined in verse 3. Since the women's hair represented her glory, the covering would be important to demonstrate her submission to man, thus maintaining God's order (I Corinthians 11:9-10). For Paul to cancel the need for a covering would not just cancel the head covering. It would also cancel the need to maintain God's order.

This is exactly what Paul is encouraging the church to maintain. This is similar to what Moses told the Jewish community in an effort to maintain God's order (Deuteronomy 22:5). Paul's focus in the passage developed through several verses should cause us to use "as" not "instead of." Another point worth making is the fact that women's hair serves as their glory, (I Corinthians 11:15) not as a sign of submission which is the point of the passage (Just think of how important it is for a woman to have her hair fixed just right). If Paul was to use women's hair as a covering, then there would be no sign of submission (again, this is one of the main points of the passage).

So for Paul to say that a woman's hair serves as a covering is to cancel the reason for writing the passage, which makes no sense especially in light of verse 5-6. "*But every woman who has her head uncovered while praying or prophesying, disgraces her head; for she is one and the same with her whose head is shaved. But if a woman does not cover her head, let her also have her hair cut off; but if it is disgraceful for a woman to have her hair cutoff or her head shaved, let her cover her head.*" Shaved head is that of a prostitute. I also believe that because women's hair served as their glory (I Corinthians 11:15), and the issue in the passage is submission that this is the reason why covering it (women's glory) when prophesying is a sign of submission. This is what Christ did (Philippians 2:6-11; I Corinthians 11:3).

Even though he is equal with God, (in this passage, I Corinthians 11:11-12, man and woman are dependent on each other and need each other) Christ stripped himself of his glory and came to earth so that mankind can receive salvation from God through him. This displacment of Christ's glory demonstrated his submission to the Father. When women put on a head covering while prophesying, they are displacing their glory for the sake of God's order in the church (I Corinthians 11:3). The reason this is such a big issue in the church is because submission is always an issue. Discussing something that is as delicate for women as their hair will always create concerns.

2. How this issue relates to male leadership in public worship:

The focus of this passage is Christ's headship (Ephesians 1:22-23; Colossians 1:18) over the Church, and how Christ's authority is transferred functionally through the man to the church. Paul is also seeking to imply that this authority does not make the man superior to the woman. This is why Paul includes that the head of Christ is God. Even though Christ submits to God, God and Christ are equal (John 10:30). In the same way, the man is the head of the woman (11:3,9), they both need each other (11:11), and are same in essence (11:12). All of this was important because women, who were once silent in the syngogues, were now an active part of worship. In order words, Paul is seeking to provide guidance as to how Christ's headship and order is maintained in the midst of a chaotic church.

Because women were prophesying when this was not the ideal situation for the church (I Corinthians 14:34; I Timothy 2:11), Paul wanted to make sure that God's creative order was not violated (11:8-9) in the church especially since the church represents the body of Christ (Eph.1:22-23). You cannot rearrange a body, while it is still living without affecting the head.

C. Analysis of the passage answers the questions outlined:

1. Is Paul telling the women to wear a head covering when they are praying or prophesying as a sign of submission to the headship of man?

Yes, I believe that Paul would like the women

despite their new found liberality to demonstrate their submission to male leadership in the church. To violate this would be to damage the distinction that God established between men and women (11:8-14). To change God's creative order will cause man to function in a disgraceful manner (11:4), and likewise women (11:5).

2. Is head covering the same as long hair?

   No, I believe that the passage explains the woman's hair as her glory (11:15), therefore the head covering (11:5-6,13) represents something completely different. It is the sign of her submission to the man (11:3).

3. Is head covering something of concern only for Paul's culture and not ours?

   Head covering meant a lot to women in Paul's culture (Historical Background, page 143-144). It determined a woman's identity, and decency. In our culture a woman covering her hair does not represent the same thing. If a woman wears a hat to church, people may perceive her as being fashionable or the pastor's wife. It does not within our culture mean that she is being submissive. Therefore, the point of the passage will not be communicated with or without head covering. The point of the passage will mostly be communicated within our culture, attached to the woman's attitude, the leadership structure, ministry structure, and bibical commitment of the church in reference to a woman teaching when men are persent.

IV. An Outline Of The Position This Passage Supports

A. The man must function in the leadership position in the church, but he is accountable to Christ through the Word (11:3).

B. Even though women are provided a lot of freedom to function in the church, they should do so in respect of male leadership especially in the area of teaching God's Word (I Corinthians 11:3-16).

C. There should be a sign of submission when a woman is exercising authority over a man (II Timothy 2:12) when teaching him in the church (11:10). If this does not occur, the woman disgraces herself (11:5-6) and presents herself as contentious (I Corinthians 11:16).

D. There should be a sign of submission for God's order when women are praying to God publicly (I Corinthians 11:13).

E. Men and women must respect the order that God created and not try to change it (I Corinthians 11:16) no matter what new principles the world provides (I Corinthians 11:2; Col. 2:8). To argue against this is to bring God's order into dispute challenging God's authority (I Corinthians 11:10).

F. Men and women are the same in essence (11:11-12) but they are different in function (11:3,7-9). Men and women compliment each other.

G. Women's hair serves as their glory (11:15). She is also the glory of her husband (11:7; Genesis 2:18-24).

H. A man should not cover his head while he is praying (11:4,7; Genesis 1:26-27).

I. If someone wants to argue with this because it is offensive to them, the church should not apologize for its position. "If anyone wants to be contentious about this, we have no other practice – nor do the churches of God" (I Corinthians 11:16-17).

Note: The key point in this passage is the headship of man and the submission of women in public worship. It is not head covering which only serves to support the focus of the passage. **This point is important for the application of this passage.**

13

The Role Of Women As It Relates To The Office Of Deacon

Introduction

There are several passages of scripture that can serve to provide clarity to this issue. However, there are two passages that are most significant to the understanding of this issue. The essential passages of scripture are I Timothy 3:8-11, and Romans 16:1. This chapter will address this issue from three positions before stating the church's position. This chapter will analyze the view that single women can serve as deaconess with the same authority as male deacons, as well as women serving only as assistance to the deacons in charge, and deaconess, women who serve along side their husbands.

An analysis of these views will hopefully provide us the opportunity to biblically crystallize the church's position on this issue. The various views to be compared will involve well-respected, trained evangelical theologians. These men, using the original languages, historical background of the text, and careful evaluate of the context, have made the decisions to be discussed.

It is because of their commitment to the text that I critically evaluate their discussion of this issue.

I. An Interpretation for Single Women Being Deaconess

A. An analysis of the word for women:

The Greek word for women is "*gynaikas*." It is pronounced goo-NAI-kas. It can mean women or wives. This word represents an adult woman or wife. There is no Greek feminine word for deaconess, just like there is no word that distinguishes a male nurse from a female nurse. Because Paul could not use a feminine word for deacon, he had to say "women" rather than deaconess.

Dr. John MacArthur, Jr. says, "The Greek word for "women" in I Timothy 3:11 is *gunaikas*. That refers, most likely, to women who are in the office of deaconess. The only way Paul could refer to women in verse 11, would be to use the Greek word *gunaikas*, because there is no feminine form of *diakonos*. The same form of the word *diakonos* is both masculine and feminine; it would have been unclear for Paul to use just the term diakonos, if he wanted to refer to women servers. He had to identify them as women."

This is important because opponents to this position state that if Paul wanted to talk about women being deacons, he would not have changed titles in verse 11. In verse two, Paul begins that section by saying, "An overseer ... ." In verse 8, Paul begins this section by saying, "Deacons likewise ... ." In the middle of this section of scripture, Paul in verse 11 says "Women must likewise ... " and then continues by stating "Let deacons be husbands of one wife ... ."

This entire section of scripture is written to describe an office. So, the opponents to this view would say, it seems that Paul would have continued to mention the office when he spoke to women in verse 11 if they too were considered to be deacons. But supporters of single women being deacons state that Paul could not do this because there is no Greek word for female deacons.

B. The use of "likewise" in Verse 11:

Dr. John MacArthur, Jr. states, "Again, the word likewise relates these women to an office of the church. It refers back to verse 1, and indicates that Paul was talking about the category of an office." Persons such as Dr. John MacArthur, Jr. state that this adverb "likewise" relates to verse 8 necessitating those women function in the same office as deacons. Opponents of this view state that "likewise" does not necessarily refer to an office of deaconess for women but could be referring to the character of the wives of deacons. This is the reason why Paul goes on to add things that he describes as unique to women (men can be double-tongued whereas women can be malicious gossips), especially since in verse 12 he will address deacons being the husbands of one wife. So since they will work together, her character is as important as his character.

C. The lack of a personal pronoun if Paul was speaking of the wives of deacons:

Dr. John MacArthur, Jr. states that "We know he wasn't talking about the wives of deacons because no pronoun was used to refer to them. If that's what he meant, he would have said their wives, or their women. And since there are no comments about the wives of elders, why would there be any comments about the wives of deacons." The opponents to this view state that mentioning "their" before wives in verse 11 was not necessary because Paul was writing to the church of Ephesus. This is the church where Paul in Ephesians 5:22-33 discusses the role of the husband as it compares with the wife. Also the absence of a pronoun may have occurred because Paul was following the pattern he had established in this section of scripture:

Verse 8: "Deacons likewise dignified"
Verse 11: "Wives likewise dignified"

"If no female deacons or women helped deacons in the church in Ephesus, the original readers would know that *gynaikas* could only be wives. Thus, the pronoun their would certainly be helpful to us, but it is not necessary to the sentence grammatically, nor was it necessary to Paul's original readers." (Strauch, Alexander. The New Testament Deacon; The Church's Minister of Mercy. Littleton, Colorado: Lewis and Roth Publishers, 1944; by page 122).

D. Single women as deacons can create structural and functional problems biblically for the supporters of this view:

Deacons provide care for hurting members, and guidance for the entire church. The church obviously involves men and women. As a result, the roles of deacons would involve providing direction in administration, caring for the needs of members, the appointment of new deacons, and assisting with the training of new deacons. In I Timothy, bear in mind that Paul is seeking to assist Timothy in setting everything in order (I Timothy 3:15).

Paul in I Timothy 1:12 states that "But I do not allow a woman to teach or exercise authority over a man, but to remain quiet." Teaching was attached to the elders in chapter 3 verse 2.

There is no mention of women in this section of scripture, which describes the role of elders. The elders and deacons were to work together to exercise authority over the body (Philippians 1:1; Hebrews 13:17). For women to function in the role of a deacon will place them in a position where they will be exercising authority over a man. Therefore Paul could not be thinking of the office of a deacon when he mentioned women in verse 11. Paul was making reference to the wives of the deacons he is describing in verse 8-10, 12-13.

"In God's design, men are to protect, lead, and provide for women, but never in a superior dominating, selfish, or belittling way. Men are to lead in a responsible, sacrificial, and loving way, like Christ does the Church" (Ephesians 5:22-33). (Strauch, Alexander. <u>The New Testament Deacon; The Church's Minister of Mercy</u>. Littleton, Colorado: Lewis and Roth Publishers, 1944; by page 119).

Supporters of this view say that women can be placed in positions such as caring for widows, single parents (who are mostly women), and single women in the church. However, opponents say that she will still be involved in meetings where decisions that affect the entire church are made.

II. An Interpretation For Women Functioning As Assistance Of Deacons

"Women must likewise be dignified, not malicious gossips, but temperate, faithful in all things" (I Timothy 3:11).

The supporters of this view state that Paul in this verse is specifically identifying a group of individuals who are workers in the church. These workers, who were women, played a significant role in the church. This is supported by passages such as Romans 16:1 where Paul commends Phoebe to the believers in Rome. It is obvious by his commendation that Phoebe played a significant role in the life of the church. This is consistent with other passages where Lydia is mentioned (Acts 16:14; the believers met at her house)

Priscilla, the wife of Aquila (Acts 18:18), and several others, not to include the Old Testament. Their roles were so significant that Paul included them to make sure they functioned in a dignified manner. Therefore, this verse is referring to women who assisted the deacons just as the deacons assisted the elders but not with the authority that comes with the position. "These women are not deacons. Yet they are so closely associated with deacons that they can be addressed within the context of deacons. These women have functions to perform or there would be no need for them to be mentioned here or to be required to meet specific qualifications. What these women do is closely associated with what deacons do. We can easily conceive of the deacons' need for women helpers to assist widows and other needy women. Thus we would assume that these women work alongside the deacons as helpers." (Strauch, Alexander. The New Testament Deacon; The Church's Minister of Mercy. Littleton, Colorado: Lewis and Roth Publishers, 1944; by page 120).

William Hendriksen, a Bible commentator, states "These women are the deacons' assistants in helping the poor and needy, etc. These are women who render auxiliary service, performing ministries for which women are better adapted." This position fits this passage as well as the examples that the New Testament and the Old Testament provides us. In the Old Testament, women helped with the temple duties. Miriam seems to have significant influence during the time of Moses. This list can continue to Ester, Rahab, etc.

In the New Testament, we have many examples, some already mentioned, such as Mary and Martha, Mary Magdalene, etc. "Now in Joppa there was a certain disciple named Tabitha (which translated in Greek is call Dorcas); this woman was abounding with deeds of kindness and charity, which she continually did" (Acts 9:36) "She extends her hand to the poor; and she stretches out her hands to the needy" (Proverbs 31:20).

III. An Interpretation For Deaconesses Being The Wives Of Deacons

A contextual analysis of the passage that seems to support this view:

When Paul begins this segment of scripture (I Timothy 3:1-15) which describes the nature of a biblical leader, he does it with direct reference being made to the office of an elder (3:2), and the office of a deacon (3:8). Verse 11 is inserted into the passage addressing an issue that is new to this passage. It seems since Paul's discussion about women is a new subject in this passage that he would have applied an office to it as he did with the others. If verse 11 was describing an office, Paul, I believe would provide the same careful description for this new office (deaconess) as he did the others. Instead, Paul mentions this in one verse and continues his discussion of a man being a deacon (vs. 12).

This verse does not begin a new section in Paul's description of leaders, as he did with elders and deacons. It is a verse in the midst of discussing who qualifies as a deacon. Therefore, Paul is not seeking to describe a new office of deaconess. He is outlining the nature of the wife who serves alongside her husband (especially since he has already written to this church about how a wife responds to her husband). This is why Paul proceeds to outline how the deacon relates to his family (vs. 12) immediately after discussing the Christian character of his wife.

This passage of scripture (3:11) is written after Paul's discussion of the role of women in the church (2:9-15) and it is written before the discussion of widows in 5:1-16, who are obviously single. So it seems since Paul has already discussed their roles, he inserts this verse to address the nature of a deacon's wife specifically, as compared to his general description of women in the passages just mentioned.

When the Corinthian church was out of order, Paul outlines the order of God (I Corinthians 11:1-3) and instructs them to follow it. In I Timothy 3:1-15, Paul states that he is writing to set things in order (vs. 15). If Paul is setting things in order, an order he addresses again in (I Timothy 2:9-15). Why would he in 3:11 violate the order he said that Christ instituted for the church? I do not believe that Paul would contradict himself especially since he repeats the order here in Timothy.

IV. Women As Deacons In The New Testament Churches

There is no recorded evidence that women served as deacons in the New Testament churches. In Acts 6:1-6, where there was a need to serve single women and widows, the apostles full of the Holy Spirit chose men. In I Timothy 5:1-16, the widows of verses 9-10 were doing a lot of work in the church; *"having a reputation for good works; and if she has brought up children, if she has shown hospitality to strangers, if she has washed the saints feet, if she has assisted those in distress, and if she has devoted herself to every good work."* Even though these women were obviously good workers, they were not functioning in the roles of deacons.

Many writers have used Romans 16:1 to prove that single women can be deacons. I'm not sure how they knew that Pheobe was single. The Greek word for deacon (*diakonos*) is used in this passage, but it is describing her as a faithful servant because of the work she provided for the body in Rome. I do not believe that Paul is mentioning this as an office. It seems if Paul was seeking to establish the office of deaconess; he would have stated it here in Romans 16:1 and explained it further in I Timothy 3:11.

V. The Deaconess And The Deacon:

An analysis of this passage supports the wife of a deacon as playing a significant role in his ministry. A deacon does not function alone in his ministry. His wife shares in his ministry. For instance, since the deacon must not be double-tongue (vs. 8), his wife must not become involved in malicious gossips (a wicked gossiper; vs. 11). Since he must be a man of dignity (vs. 8), then she must be a woman who is dignified (vs. 11). After Paul addresses the nature of the wife, he immediately begins discussions on the role of the deacon as a manager of his home. How the wife assists her husband with this function is outlined in chapter 5 verse 14 (this completes what Paul means when he says faithful in all things; 5:9-10). Because a deacon is not required to teach, and he serves under the elders, his wife serving along side him supports his position in the church as outlined by Paul in 2:9-15.

14

Tongues And The Manifestation Of The Holy Spirit In The Life Of A Believer

There are many things said about tongues and the manifestation of the Holy Spirit in the life of a believer. This is sometimes a result of inept study or just a repeat of information heard without a proper examination of the subject. The purpose of this study is to examine this issue from a biblio-centric perspective. It is not to refute or create controversy or division among us but to objectively evaluate what is consistent with the Word of God.

I. Tongues: Is It A Spirit-Filled Gift For The Church Today?

There are only seven passages in the entire Bible that address this issue. The passages are Isaiah 28:11-12 and Joel 2:28, which find its context in verses 19-32. It was quoted by Peter in Acts

2:16-21. Other passages related to this subject are Mark 16:17, Acts 2:10,19 and I Corinthians 12-14. We will seek to address each one as it relates to this subject.

II. Definition of Tongues:

1. Tongues is from the Greek word *glossa* which refers either to the physical organ or to a language. This is found in I Corinthians 14:18; Acts 2 and I Corinthians 12-14.

2. Another word related to tongues which was used in Acts 2 is "*dialect*". This again refers to a known language.

3. *Unknown tongues* is mentioned in I Corinthians 13:1. This is a language that is not of this world. However, the word "unknown" is added to the King James Version which is why it is italicized. In this passage, Paul states that speaking in a tongue that is not a known language is "only a resounding gong or a clanging cymbal." In other words, it was meaningless. Also, there were pagan religions in Corinth that were using meaningless chatter as a form of worship. I believe; this is why Paul told the church in Corinth to get interpreters (I Corinthians 14:13, 27), to steer them away from meaningless chatter. Therefore, I Corinthians 13:1 cannot be used to prove that Paul is advocating meaningless, ecstatic speech or some kind of heavenly or angelic message.

4. *Tongue* (singular use in I Corinthians 14:2): The context shows that Paul is focused on the fact that spiritual gifts are not for personal edification but it is focused on building others up. So if someone was to speak in an unknown tongue, they are using their gift for their own personal benefit and not the benefit of the body. That is not the purpose of a gift. It is quite obvious that Paul (I Corinthians) and Luke (Acts) were speaking of a known language not meaningless chatter, which we find much of today. The use of tongues was a sign of Israel's rejection of the truth (Isaiah 28:11-12), and God's desire to reach the lost throughout the world (Acts 2).

III. Analysis of Passages Mentioned Above:

1. Isaiah 28:11-12: This passage serves as a rebuke to Israel's leaders for their refusal to listen to Isaiah. Because these leaders refuse to listen to Isaiah, God through Isaiah, states that he will speak to them in Gentile tongues. So what occurred in Acts 2:4,6 serves as a condemnation to Israel because of their lack of respect for God's Word as well as Jesus Christ. They nailed him to a cross.

2. Joel 2:28: Many Pentecostals believe that this passage is being fulfilled today. Some Pentecostals who believe that tongues may have ceased, says it is now alive for the church today. Evangelicals, people who are not Pentecostals, believe that

Peter mentioned this passage because it was partially fulfilled at Pentecost. And it will not be totally fulfilled until the tribulation period, so it is future. Just like the Transfiguration experience gave a preview of the glory to come, so Pentecost gave a preview of the gathering of Israel in the last days. Evangelicals believe for the following reasons:

a. Joel 2:20 is referring to the defeat of the northern kingdom called Israel in the end-times. Because it talks about wonders in the sky and on the earth blood, fire and columns of smoke: "The sun will be turned into darkness, and the moon into blood, before the great and awesome day of the Lord comes" (v.31) <u>none of this occured at Pentecost.</u>

b. Joel 2:27 talks about a revival that will bring Israel back to God. This is not yet fulfilled.

c. Joel 3 is talking about judgement that will come upon nations after the battle of Armageddon, which will be a battle of Satan forces and God's.

d. Joel 2 talks about the millennial kingdom which is obviously not fulfilled.

3. Mark 16:17

a. Mark was making reference to the apostles.

b. All of these powerful miracles were fulfilled by the apostles while on earth. In the latter church before the end of the New Testament age there were few or no miracles being performed.

c. In James, healing came as a result of the elders of the church praying for the believer.

4. Acts 2:1-13: We have already discussed this passage and came to the following conclusions: The word tongues used in verse 4 was tied to dialect in verse 6, so this was a known language provided to the disciples.

5. Acts 10:44-48 (Peter reports this incident in Acts 11:17 & 15:7-9):

   a. There was a manifestation of the Holy Spirit first because they accepted Christ into their hearts. Tongues came later because I believe this was truly the only way Peter's jewish companions as well as, Peter himself, would really believe that the Gentiles' brothers were saved. Christ had to give Peter a vision and the Holy Spirit had to command him (Acts 10:1-29) before he would even consider going to Cornelius' house. Speaking in tongues in the same manner as occurred for the apostles was the best way Christ could convince Peter that he (Christ) would save the Gentiles. This is repeated by Peter on the following occasions: Acts 10:45: "And all the circumcised believers who had come with Peter were amazed, because the gift of the Holy Spirit had been poured out upon the Gentiles also."

b. Acts 10:47: "Surely no one can refuse the water for these to be baptized who have received the Holy Spirit just as we did, can he?"

1. In Paul's case, this manifestation was not necessary. Paul went to one place after another and Gentiles accepted Christ, but there was no such manifestation (Acts 19:1-7) because it was clear to Paul that his ministry was to the Gentiles (Acts 9: 15-16).

2. In the passage above, it is clear that this is a known language.

6. Acts 19:1-7: **Question**: Does it take the laying on of hands to receive the Holy Spirit after accepting Christ as Savior?

a. When Paul placed his hands on them, this was another significant time in church history (just like it was for Peter in the passage above) because Ephesus was a new center of the Gentile mission – the next in importance after

Syrian Antioch. These 12 disciples were to be the nucleus of the Ephesian Church (Acts 19:9,10;20:13-38).

b. This had to be a significant event because there are several other times in Acts that the apostles placed their hands on someone or individuals and they did not speak in tongues (Acts 6:6; 13:3; 9:17). The Acts 9:17 passage is a significant demonstration of this. Because it states when Ananias placed his hands on Paul, he was filled with the Holy Spirit but he did not speak in tongues.

c. Just as above tongues mentioned in the passages is a known language.

7. I Corinthians 12-14: There are several points in these passages which highlight Paul's desire to have less emphasis placed on tongues in the Corinthian church. These points are as follows:

a. Paul viewed tongues as one of the lesser gifts (I Corinthians 12:31).

b. Tongues that are unintelligible words do not edify the body (I Corinthians 14:4, 9-17).

c. Paul did not view tongues as important for church worship service (I Corinthians 14:18-19).

d. Tongues were for unbelievers, so what use is it for believers in a church service (I Corinthians 12:21-22).

e. Those who make tongues an important part of the church are thinking like children (I Corinthians 13:8-12; 14:20).

f. Unintelligible words will not reach an unbeiever, it would drive them away (I Corinthians 14:23-24).

g. One of the reasons Paul discouraged tongues is that it created confusion (I Corinthians 14:9, 16,23,33).

8. Tongues will cease (I Corinthians 13:1-8):

a. In this passage, it is clear that Paul is saying that we need to focus on the development of christian character which is demonstrated by our love for one another (John 13:35) rather than the less important things which will cease (cease means to permanently stop).

b. For a believer to continue to cause division and confusion in the church rather than love one another is to behave like a child (vs. 11-12).

9. Tongues and New Testament history:

a. Tongues were a sign symbolizing the curse of God on a disobedient nation (Isaiah 28:11) as well as God providing salvation to the unbelieving Gentiles (I Corinthians 14:21-22). Tongues therefore became a sign of transition between the Old Testament and the New Testament.

b. Tongues is only recorded in the early books in the New Testament (Acts and I Corinthians), but it is never mentioned in the later books.

c. Tongues were never mentioned in:

I or II Peter, James, John's books, Jude, Ephesians, Colossians, Philippians, Romans, etc. All later books did not discuss tongues. It never seem to be an issue in later churches.

d. By the time of the Pastoral Epistles Paul told Timothy to find faithful men and teach them and then encourage them to teach others (II Timothy 2:2). There is no mention for these men to have the gift of tongues.

e. By the time of Hebrews (Hebrews 2:3-4), signs and wonders were seen as something in the past tied to the apostles.

f. I Corinthians was written in A.D. 55, but when II Corinthians was written in A.D. 56,

1 years later, there is no mention of signs, just a key verse 12:12; *"The signs of a true apostle* ***were*** *performed among you with all perseverance, by signs and wonders and miracles."*

g. "The last recorded miracles in the New Testament occurred around A.D. 58, with the healings on the Island of Malta (Acts 28:7-10). From A.D. 96 to 58, when John finished the book of Revelation, no miracle is recorded." (John McCarther, Charismatic Chaos, page 282).

IV. How Do We Know We Are Filled With The Spirit?

We know we are filled when the following occurs:

1. There is an active demonstration of the fruit of the Spirit (Galatians 5:22-26).

2. We develop an appetite for the Word of God (John 16:13; I John 5:6; I Peter 2:2-3)

3. The person's life will demonstrate the life of Christ (Luke 6:43; Matthew 7:16; 12:33; Philippians 1:11).

4. Anyone who accepts that Jesus is truly the Messiah and when tested proves to be true (I John 4:1-3).

5. Anyone who does not continually sin with no de-

sire for repentance (I John 5:18-20).

6. Demonstrates a willingness to obey the Word of God (Acts 5:32).

Conclusion

Tongues is definitely a spiritual gift provide by God through the Holy Spirit. The purpose for tongues was more for evangelism than for the worship environment.When various tongues were spoken in the church at Corinth, Paul did not encouarge it for the worship service (I Corinthians 14). Because it edified the individual speaking in tongues, the congregation looks like they were out of their minds.We must be more focus on developing the fruits of the Spirit (Galatians 5:22-26) because they develop the character of believers and they bless those they (believers) impact on a daily basis.It is for this purpose that Christ said that we must abide in him. By abiding in him we will be able to bear much fruits (John 15:1-10).

15

Teaching Our Youth By Critiquing Secular Material

Introduction

The purpose of this discussion is to examine whether or not we will be functioning outside of the will of God by allowing our youth to biblically critique secular lyrics while listening to them.

I. Foundational Issues That Must Examined

We must examine the following issues:

A. How does Christ want us to function relevant to the secular world?

B. What are some of the issues that would cause Christ to remove himself from the church?

C. Did Christ ever use the negative customs of the world to teach and explain his way?

D. If Paul says, "All things are lawful for me, but not all things are profitable ... ." the question becomes since all things are lawful, what is not profitable?

E. Does teaching our youth from a negative and worldly vantage point promote false doctrine in the church?

II. Biblical Examination Of The Issues

Each of the questions outlined above is carefully examined and then summarized in an effort to formulate the position of the Church.

A. How does Christ wants us to function relevant to the secular world?

The Bible views Satan as the ruler of the world (John 14:30; I John 5:19), someone seeking to devour believers (I Peter 5:8), and destroy God's sheep (John 10:10). Therefore, anything that is promoted by the world that is evil comes from Satan. The Bible says all good things come from above (James 1:17). It is Christ and Satan who are opposed to one another (Ephesians 6:11-12; I John 4:4) with Christ already having all authority in his hands (Matthew 28:18).

Christ instructs believers not to love the world because Satan is the ruler of the world. In I John 2:15-16, the Bible says "*Do not love the world, nor the things in the world. If anyone loves the world, the love of the Father is not in him. For all that is in the world, the lust of the flesh and the lust of the eyes and the boastful pride of life, is not from the Father, but is from the world.*" This is why Christ states through James that anyone who loves the world becomes an enemy of God (John 4:4). This can be in the form of things in the world that are contrary to God's Word, or the love of money (Matthew 6:24; I Timothy 6:7-10).

This love-for-the-world attitude is what allows us, even though we are saved to be opposed to God and causes Christ to not be for us (Romans 8:31). Christ does not expect us to not function in the world each day. He simply does not want us to love the things of the world and become involved in following the lust of the flesh. Christ states in John 17:15-18; "*I do not ask Thee to take them out of the world, but to keep them from the evil one. They are not of the world, even as I am not of the world. Sanctify them in the truth. Thy word is truth. As Thou didst send Me into the world. I also have sent them into the world.*"

The emphasis in these verses is to allow believers to exist in the world while being sanctified through the Word of God. This is why Paul would say in Romans 12:2, "*And do not be conformed to this world, but be transformed by the renewing of your mind, that you may prove what the will of God is, that which is good and acceptable and perfect.*" Therefore, we are not expected to live in isolation of the world. We must live as an active part of the world while being transformed into the image of God (II Corinthians 3:18), so that we can be a light to the world drawing the unbeliever to Christ (Matthew 5:14-16; 28:19-20).

B. Issues that would cause Christ to remove himself from the church:

Revelation 2-3 discusses why Christ will remove his lampstand (Christ's presence) from the churches. The following are those reasons:

1. The believers in the Church of Ephesus were no longer loving one another (Revelation 2:4-6).

2. The believers in the Church of Smyrna must be willing to endure suffering for Christ (Revelation 2:10-11).

3. The believers in the Church of Pergamum were promoting a false doctrine, the doctrine of Balaam (Revelation 2:14-15). They were not teaching against it.

4. The believers in the Church of Thyatira were promoting a false doctrine. They were not teaching against it (Revelation 2:20-25).

5. The believers in the Church of Sardis were not serving the Lord completely (Revelation 2:1-3).

6. The believers in the Church of Philadelphia were blessed for holding to the truth (Revelation 2:8-11).

7. The believers in the Church of Laodicea served God halfheartedly. They were serving Christ in a manner that was called "luke-warm" and Christ rejects them for this (Revelation 2:15-20).

The reasons these churches were rejected are because they were not loving one another (I John 4:7-12). They refused to serve Christ wholeheartedly, and they continually taught false doctrine. I Timothy 4:1-2,7 says; *"But the Spirit explicitly says that in later times some will fall away from the faith, paying attention to deceitful spirits and doctrines of demons, by means of the hypocrisy of liars seared in their own conscience as with a branding iron. But have nothing to do with worldly fables fit only for old women. On the other hand, discipline yourself for the purpose of godliness."* This doctrine was promoted in the church and the pastors in the church did not speak out against it. Therefore, Christ removed himself from these churches. This passage also instructs us to discipline ourselves for the purpose of godliness (II Peter 1:3-11).

C. Did Christ ever use the negative customs of the world to teach and explain his way?

There are several occurrences of Christ using the negative to reinforce the positive. We will examine five examples of Christ using the negative customs of the Jews to teach his disciples:

1. In Matthew 6:5-8, Christ refers to the hypocrites who would pray to impress people around them. He uses this custom to teach the disciples how they should not pray.

2. In Matthew 6:16-18, Christ refers to hypocrites who would do everything possible to let everyone know that they were fasting in order to impress people around them. Christ instructs the disciples to not imitate this custom.

3. In Luke 18:9-14, Christ refers to the Pharisees who would go to the temple and boastfully pray. Christ explains this custom in order to teach the disciples how they should humble themselves before God when they pray.

4. Christ explains the situation concerning a wicked manager to teach believers how individuals in the world function as better stewards than Christians (Luke 16:1-9).

5. Jesus teaches the disciples about forgiveness by sharing the story about the unmerciful/wicked servant (Matthew 18:21-35).

Christ came and taught us because he knew that we were slaves to the knowledge and ways of the world rather than to his Word (Galatians 4:3-4). He desired to renew our minds (Romans 12:2) so that he could transform our lives. Therefore, Christ used what was normally occurring to explain what he wanted us to know (Colossians 2:20-3:17; II Peter 2:10-21). In the Old Testament, God allowed Gomer to become a prostitute to teach Israel how their worship of other gods caused them to prostitute themselves before God.

Paul followed this pattern when he went into the temple to teach and found an inscription "to an unknown god" (Acts 17:23). Paul used this inscription to introduce the "Men of Athens" to our Lord and Savior Jesus Christ. Perhaps this is why Paul said in I Corinthians 9:22, *"To the weak; I have become all things to all men, that I may by all means save some. And I do all things for the sake of the gospel, that I may become a fellow partaker of it."*

It was Paul who said that "*...God has chosen the foolish things of the world to shame the wise, and God has chosen the weak things of the world to shame the things which are strong, and the base things of the world and the despised, God has chosen the things that are not, that he might nullify the things that are.*" (I Corinthians 1:26-28; same thought is in verse 20-21.) These are some of the instances in scripture where Jesus used the negative to highlight the importance of the positive.

D. If Paul says "*all things are lawful for me, but not all things are profitable ....,*" The question becomes since all things are lawul, what is not profitable? (I Corinthians 6:12).

The reason that Paul wrote this particular verse was because the Corinthians were saying that they were free to do whatever they wanted to do. Paul responded by stating that they were free to do whatever they wanted to, but not everything they did was beneficial for the sake of Christ. Paul explained this by talking about food, and immorality, immediately after having discussed lawsuits, homosexuality, and that thieves, the greedy, drunkards, slanderers, and swindlers shall not inherit the kingdom of God. In other words, people could be any of these things, but this was not profitable. It did not lead to mutual edification (Romans 14:19), and it could hurt a weak brother (Romans 14:1-8; 15:1-4).

Therefore, even though we have the freedom to do all things, we must focus on doing those things that are beneficial for the body (Colossians 3:1-4).

E. Does teaching our youth from a negative and worldly vantage point promote false doctrine in the church?

The promotion of false doctrine occurred when false teachers were allowed to teach in the church (I Timothy 4:1-5; Revelation 2), and no one sought to stop them. These false teachers promoted what they believed as though was truth. They also sought to cause the church to be guided by what they taught rather than the sound doctrine taught to the church by the apostles. When we allow our youth to listen to the lyrics of secular songs (stopping the tape to discuss each verse), we are not encouraging them to obey what they are probably already listening to; we are seeking to teach why they should not listen to it.

Therefore, we are not promoting false doctrine. We are seeking to discipline them for the purpose of living godly lives in a lawless world. For our leaders to teach young people false doctrine will lead to severe punishment for us (Revelation 2; Christ takes his lampstand) and for the leaders (Matthew 5:19-20; 18:5-6); *"And whoever receives one such child in my name receives me; but whoever causes one of these little ones who believe in me to stumble, it is better for him that a heavy millstone be hung around his neck, and that he be drowned in the depth of the sea."*

III. Summary Of All The Issues Discussed

We can summarize the answers to the questions, addressed in this chapter, in the following manner:

A. Christ did use the negative customs of his day to encourage his followers to understand the importance of functioning biblically in a lawless world.

B. Christ did not tolerate the church promoting false doctrine. Anything that was being taught that was not in line with teachings of Christ and the apostles was not to be tolerated in the church. To allow someone to teach false doctrine whether in small groups or large was in violation of God's Word. The results for allowing this were severe.

C. The Word of God allows us the freedom to play this music when the purpose is to teach our youth why listening to ungodly music can stunt their spiritual growth. We are playing the music (being constantly shut off and on) to teach young people what is wrong with it; therefore, we are not promoting what it is teaching thereby allowing false doctrine into the church.

I do not believe however, that the playing of the music should occur in the sanctuary. The Gentiles were allowed in the other courts in the Old Testament, but they were not allowed in the inner courts because they had no covenant with God and would have defiled the temple. To allow this music into the sanctuary, a place where we collectively worship Christ, would defile it. We are not, by playing this music in a classroom, promoting false doctrine because we are using this music as a method of teaching our youth about what is wrong. So we are using the negative to promote the positive biblical principles of God's Word.

16

The Church's Response To Social Injustice

I. Introduction

The topic of God's call on the church is broad. This chapter addresses one specific issue: How should the church respond to social injustice? First, a hypothetical example is given. Second, relevant scripture is offered and considered. Next, a practical policy is presented. Finally, the hypothetical problem is revisited.

The Christian has both individual and corporate responsibilities. The individual responsibilities flow from our one-to-one relationship with Christ. Individually, each person comes alone to Christ and is called to follow him. Once saved, each also becomes part of a larger body, the Bride of Christ, the "invisible" Church made up of all those who are born-again. Our corporate responsibilities flow from our membership in Christ's church. The ideal local church is a tiny portion of the larger "invisible" Church (even though important to its overall existence) and accepts the responsibilites God has placed on it as part of that blessed group.

The problem may be illustrated by an example:

An elderly widow, on a low-fixed income lives alone in a small apartment. She has lived there for several years, is a good tenant, and pays her rent on time. For several months, the roof has leaked every time it rains. She has complained to the manager several times, but he never fixed the leak. Finally, she filed a complaint with the city. As soon as the complex manager was notified of the complaint, he sent her an eviction notice. She told him that he was being unfair. He said, "So sue me. If you aren't out in ten days I'll throw your junk on the curb." She has no money to move and nowhere to go. She goes to the church and asks for help.

II. A Biblical Exposition Of This Subject

A. The Old Testament:

Although the Old Testament was written before the Church was established, its principles and examples can serve as an example for the church on the issue. It was Paul who said what took place in the Old Testament was a shadow of things to come (Colossians 2:16-17). Even though we are evaluating this in the Old Testament, we will continue to link this to the New Testament passages so that the transition process is well structured.

The law of God was divided into three areas; the ceremonial law, the moral law and the civil law. The ceremonial law is now tied into the life of Christ (Ephesians 2:13-22) who serves as our high priest (Hebrews 8:1-6). *"Do not think that I came to abolish the Law or the Prophets; I did not come to abolish but to fulfill. For truly I say to you, until heaven and earth pass away, not the smallest letter or stroke shall pass from the Law until all is accomplished. Whoever then annuls one of the least of these commandments, and teaches others to do the same, shall be called least in the kingdom of heaven; but whoever keeps and teaches them, he shall be called great in the kingdom of heaven"* (Matthew 5:17-19). The civil and moral laws still exist and God expects us to respect them (Deutronomony and Romans 13). As a result, there are many things that we can learn from the civil and moral laws of God that can be applied to the church today.

Christ serves as the transition from the Old Testament to the New Testament in that he came to fulfill the law not abolish it (Matthew 5:17-19; quoted above). The Israelites were under a theocracy, the direct rule of God. He expressed his will through scripture and his chosen leaders and prophets. This was not provided to any other nation so it would be impossible for the Gentiles to dispense justice when there was no just law among them. Only those who know the truth can stand for the truth.

This is the same for the New Testament Church; "*but in case I am delayed, I write so that you may know how one ought to conduct himself in the household of God, the pillar and support of the truth"* (I Timothy 3:15). "*And He put all things in subjection under His feet, and gave Him as head over all things to the church, which is His body, the fulness of Him who fills all in all"* (Ephesians 1:22-23). The implementation of the law was totally dependent on the people of God as a model to the world. *"And I will bless those who bless you, and the one who curses you I will curse. And in you all the families of the earth shall be blessed"* (Genesis 12:1-3). This responsibility required God to provide specific guidelines relevant to the moral and civil laws for the smooth operation of Israel as a nation unto God.

There are numerous references to social injustice in the Old Testament. Most of the references are warnings against being unjust to others in the Jewish community. There are also promises of God's judgment against the unjust which was due to the lack of justice among the people of Israel for the poor, the orphan, the widow and the needy. They can be found throughout the book of Exodus and Deutronomony. Even though some of the passages instruct Israel to respond to injustice that was done to its citizens, we can relate this to the church who is a nation unto God.

"But you are A CHOSEN RACE, A royal PRIESTHOOD, A HOLY NATION, A PEOPLE FOR God's OWN POSSESSION, so that you may proclaim the excellencies of Him who has called you out of darkness into His marvelous light; for you once were NOT A PEOPLE, but now you are THE PEOPLE OF GOD; you had NOT RECEIVED MERCY, but now you have RECEIVED MERCY" (I Peter 2:9-10). We are just as responsible to function as a nation unto God since we are provided the rule of God, God's Word (Hebrews 1:1-4), for the world (Ephesians 1:22-23). Just as Israel's behavior, before they acted sinfully, became an example for God throughout the world, so the church's response to this issue can become an example to the secular community. *"Proclaim on the citadels in Ashdod and on the citadels (citadels was used as the last place of defense when an enemy broke through the walls of a city) in the land of Egypt and say, "Assemble youselves on the mountains of Samaria and see the great tumults within her and the oppressions in her midst. But they do not know how to do what is right," declares the Lord, "these who hoard up violence and devastation in their citadels."* (Amos 3:9-10). *"For it is time for judgment to begin with the household of God; and if it begins with us first, what will be the outcome for those who do not obey the gospel of God?"* (I Peter 4:17).

Isaiah 1:17 provides straight forward counsel concerning how to take an active role to help victims. It instructs us "*to seek justice, reprove the ruthless, (scripture is writen for this purpose II Timothy 3:16), defend the orphan, plead for the widow."* The emphasis here is to seek justice thus stressing the individual responsibility of the members of Israel. The nation is expected to work in a cooperative manner to achieve justice for those who need help such as the orphans, widows, the poor or anyone who is treated in an unjust manner. God has a sincere love for the poor; *"He will have compassion on the poor and needy, and the lives of the needy he will save"* (Psalm 72:13). The same attitude of compassion was expected from believers in the New Testament as an attribute of Christ (Philippians 2:1-5; Colossians 3:12).

Jeremiah 5:28-29 promises judgment against those who do not come to the aid of abused orphans and the poor. That is, it declares an obligation to help not just a prohibition against causing harm. We may consider failure to help the weak a sin of omission. *"They are fat, they are sleek, they also excel in deeds of wickedness; They do not plead the cause, the cause of the orphan, that they may prosper; And they do not defend the rights of the poor. 'Shall I not punish these people?' declares the Lord, 'On a nation such as this shall I not avenge myself?'"* (Jeremiah 5:28-29). Jeremiah is stating that because the people did not seek for justice as God had instructed; God is going to judge them as if he is avenging himself. This is why Zechariah 7:9-10 says, *"Thus has the LORD of hosts said, 'Dispense true justice and practice kindness and compassion each to his brother; and do not oppress the widow or the orphan, the stranger or the poor; and do not devise evil in your hearts against one another.'"*

Like the Jeremiah and Zechariah verses above, Amos 5:15 directs the active establishment of justice. *"Hate evil, love good, and establish justice in the gate! Perhaps the Lord God of hosts may be gracious to the remnant of Joseph."* Amos continues by saying, *"But let justice roll down like waters And righteousness like an ever-flowing stream"* (Amos 5:24). Because God expects the nation of Israel to respond to injustice, the obedience of individuals therefore the obedience of a nation allows his God's justice (since it is based on his Word) to flow freely.

God states repeatedly that the needs of the poor must be addressed. To not address the needs of the poor causes God to respond with justice for the injustice. Here are some examples:

1. God expects the poor to be defended when cheated in business matters (Amos 8:4-6). Again God has to avenge the needy because the people did not do anything.

2. When members of Israel turn the poor aside at the city gates (Amos 5:12), the leaders and the other citizens of Israel did nothing about it. The New Testament addresses this by instructing the Thessalonians to confront the unruly and help the weak (I Thessalonians 5:14). Paul tells the Romans to contribute *"to the needs of the saints, practicing hospitality…"* (Romans 12:13). Practicing hospitality is one of the qualifications for an elder (I Timothy 3:2).

Except for Isaiah 1:17, the process described above challenges the members of the Jewish community to not allow injustice to continue unchecked within the nation. The Bible states that this is where it must start before injustice is properly addressed in the community, meaning the unsaved (I Peter 4:17). *"Does any one of you, when he has a case against his neighbor, dare to go to law before the unrighteous and not before the saints? Or do you not know that the saints will judge the world? If the world is judged by you, are you not competent to constitute the smallest law courts? Do you not know that we will judge angels? How much more matters of this life?"* (I Corinthians 6:1-3). God expected the church to serve as an example to the world of how to deal with these matters because it is the church that has the whole counsel of God (Acts 20:27; 2 Peter 1:3-4).

The nation of Israel in the wilderness, before ever going into the Promised Land, became a self-sufficient nation even though it had no clothing, food stores or other support mechanisms we have today. The people functioned as a community unto God, led by God's laws and sustained by God's power. The poor did not die of hunger and Moses allowed God's laws to create justice for the nation. Even during a time of chaos when Deborah ruled as a civil judge, it was the moral and civil laws of God that kept the nation from being totally torn apart. In the Book of Judges, once the nation was committed to function under the just rule of God; it became empowered to fight those who practiced injustice against them. This supports I Peter 4:17 and I Corinthians 6:1-3 (quoted above).

The church is expected, internally or externally, to address these issues. After all, Isaiah tells us that it is for this purpose Christ came, *"Then a shoot will spring from the stem of Jesse, and a branch from his roots will bear fruit. The Spirit of the LORD will rest on him, the spirit of wisdom and understanding, the spirit of counsel and strength, the spirit of knowledge and the fear of the LORD. And he will delight in the fear of the LORD, and he will not judge by what his eyes see, nor make a decision by what his ears hear; But with righteousness He will judge the poor, and decide with fairness for the afflicted of the earth; And he will strike the earth with the rod of his mouth, and with the breath of his lips he will slay the wicked. Also righteousness will be the belt about his loins, and faithfulness the belt about his waist"* (Isaiah 11:1-5). *"The Spirit of the Lord GOD is upon me, because the LORD has anointed me to bring good news to the afflicted; he has sent me to bind up the brokenhearted, to proclaim liberty to captives and freedom to prisoners"* (Isaiah 61:1).

Again, nowhere does God says they were to go out and fight against injustice except during the time of the judges when God removed them from the oppression of their neighbors. God made it clear, that as a nation, he expected them to uphold his word and to love their neighbor as themselves. If they obeyed God then justice would flow like a river whether this occurred internally or externally. This process would then become an example to all nations. It is this example that becomes the power of influence to the Gentiles.

Summary:

1. The principles taught by Old Testament civil and moral laws are still functional today.

2. The rule of God is still important to the church as it was to the nation of Israel. It can therefore provide direction as the church addresses current social injustice issues.

3. Like Israel, the church is viewed as a nation unto God and is expected to be an example of God to the world.

4. As individual members of the nation of God, we are responsible to respond to social injustice.

5. Because we are a nation unto God and he has clearly instructed us to fight for the orphan, the widow, the poor and the needy, we have the power through his Word to fight for injustice.

B. The New Testament:

The Church began on the Pentecost following Christ's ascension. The gospels and various other passages speak of events prior to the church. Portions of the epistles and Revelation speak directly about the church.

1. Christ foretold the church but provided few details of how the church functions cooperatively (Paul is the key figure that outlines this for us). His recorded words and works primarily tell us how he came to demonstrate his authority, to sacrifice himself for us, to conquer death, and to give eternal life to those who trust him. He spoke of our duty to do good and to love others but not of a corporate fight against injustice. There are several examples of how Christ exposed this for us. Here are a few:

    a) On several occasions, Christ opposed the Pharisees and Sadducees for the way they treated people who abuse the law based on their interpretation of the law (John 8:1-11; Luke 7:36-39). The Scribes and Pharisees were quick to bring the woman before Christ for her sin without taking into account their own sin. They did the same thing in Luke 7:36-39. This is why Christ stated that before someone can address the speck in his brother's eye he must deal with the log in his own eye (Matthew 7:1-6). This process insures that justice is true justice and not hypocritical. How could a Police Officer stop someone for drugs when he sold them the drugs a block away?

b) When Jesus cleansed the temple by turning over the money tables, he again addressed injustice. The Jewish people traveled for miles with animals working hard to keep them undefiled before God, only to arrive at the temple to be told that they were not clean. They then had to go outside to get an animal where a lot of money was demanded not only to purchase the animal but to exchange their money to the needed currency. When this was the only way they could have sins forgiv-forgiven, each person was placed in a very difficult situation. This made things extremly difficult for the poor.

c) When the disciples wanted to send home the people who had followed Christ all day, Jesus took care of a social need by feeding five thousand people (John 6:1-14).

d) When Jesus healed the woman with the issue of blood, he exposed the woman before everyone because everyone had to know about her blood flow. She could not go to the temple to be cleansed because this was a continual problem for years. This was a flow of blood, so many people may have come to know about it. If they touched her, they could not go to the temple for several days. They did not want to be unclean. This is most likely why she could make her way through a crowd that was pressing against Jesus (Mark 5:24, 31). Jesus publicly told the woman she was well before everyone establishing her back into her community.

e) Jesus again showed a concern for social issues when he said the following to believers after the rapture: *"Then the King will say to those on His right, 'Come, you who are blessed of My Father, inherit the kingdom prepared for you from the foundation of the world. For I was hungry, and you gave Me something to eat; I was thirsty, and you gave Me something to drink; I was a stranger, and you invited Me in; naked, and you clothed Me; I was sick, and you visited Me; I was in prison, and you came to Me.' Then the righteous will answer Him, 'Lord, when did we see You hungry, and feed You, or thirsty, and give You something to drink? And when did we see You a stranger, and invite You in, or naked, and clothe You? When did we see You sick, or in prison, and come to You?' The King will answer and say to them, 'Truly I say to you, to the extent that you did it to one* *of these brothers of Mine, even the least of them, you did it to Me"'* (Matthew 25:34-40).

f) The reason for this focus that is centered on the church community is because this is the very purpose for which Jesus came. *"THE SPIRIT OF THE LORD IS UPON ME, BECAUSE HE ANOINTED ME TO PREACH THE GOSPEL TO THE POOR. HE HAS S ENT ME TO PROCLAIM RELEASE TO THE CAPTIVES, AND RECOVERY OF SIGHT TO THE BLIND, TO SET FREE THOSE WHO ARE OPPRESSED, TO PROCLAIM THE FAVORABLE YEAR OF THE LORD"* (Luke 4:18-19).

Jesus did not tell the church to cooperatively fight against social injustice but he did model as Head of the Church, who is his body the pillar and foundation of all truth (I Timothy 5:15), previously how it should respond to social injustice. His mission as stated was to care for the oppressed and he demonstrated this when he fought for the poor, told the story of the Good Samaritan, drank from the cup of the Samaritan woman, healed the sick, helped the man who could not get into the pool to be healed, corrected Zacheus, and saved the thief on the cross.

Because believers are the salt and light of the world (Matthew 5:13-16), how we function as a nation unto God (I Peter 2:9-10) becomes the model that the world can imitate. The church must create the climate that the whole world adjusts to.

2. The books of Acts and the epistles give us some information about the organization and and function of the church but primarily address the responsibility of the members of the church to one another. There is no strong call for the church to coorperatively oppose social injustice perpetrated by non-believers. Still, it is expected to function in a manner that creates social norms that highlight the character of God.

   a) Peter was eating with the Gentiles when the Jews walked in. When he saw the Jews, he left the Gentiles and went to the Jews. Paul confronted his hypocrisy. *"But when Cephas came to Antioch, I opposed him to his face, because he stood condemned. For prior to the coming of certain men from James, he used to eat with the Gentiles; but when they came, he began to withdraw and hold himself aloof, fearing the party of the circumcision. The rest of the Jews joined him in hypocrisy, with the result that even Barnabas was carried away by their hypocrisy. But when I saw that they were not straightforward about the truth of the gospel, I said to Cephas in the presence of all, "If you, being a Jew, live like the Gentiles and not like the Jews, how is it that you compel the Gentiles to live like Jews?"* (Galatians 2:11-14).

   b) We see a similar situation in the book of James where the rich were being treated better than the poor. James addresses this issue by saying, *"Listen, my beloved brethren: did not God choose the poor of this world to be rich in faith and heirs of the kingdom which He promised to those who love Him? But you have dishonored the poor man. Is it not the rich who oppress you and personally drag you into court? Do they not blaspheme the fair name by which you have been called? If, however, you are fulfilling the royal law according to the Scripture, "YOU SHALL LOVE YOUR NEIGHBOR AS YOURSELF," you are doing well. But if you show partiality, you are committing sin and are convicted by the law as transgressors"* (James 2:5-9).

3. Notwithstanding the above, we know from the words and works of Christ and from the epistles that it is our individual and coorper ate responsibility to love and treat everyone, both fairly the lost and the born-again. In particular, we are responsibile to love and help our fellow brothers and sisters in Christ, members of Christ's Church.

a) In John 13:34-35, Jesus called us to love one another not only because it is right but also as a witness to the world. *"A new commandment I give to you, that you love one another, even as I have loved you, that you also love one another. By this all men will know that you are My disciples, if you have love for one another."*

b) In Acts, we learn how the members of the early church held all things in common, for the common good, so that none would go without. *"And all those who had believed were together and had all things in common; and they began selling their property and possessions and were sharing them with all, as anyone might have need."* (Acts 2: 44-45) *"And the congregation of those who believed were of one heart and soul; and not one of them claimed that anything belonging to him was his own, but all things were common property to them"* (Acts 4:32).

c) In I Thessalonians 5:14 we are told to help the weak. *"We urge you, brethren, admonish the unruly, encourage the fainthearted, help the weak, be patient with everyone."*

4. Paul's insistence that his rights as a Roman citizen be recognized gives us a scriptural example of a stand against governmental injustice. This is chronicled in the last half of the book of Acts, (Acts 21-28).

5. Individuals should first look to their own abilities and assets before turning to the church for help.

a) Paul said in II Thessalonians 3:10 that if a person would not work, he should not eat. *"For even when we were with you, we used to give you* *this order: if anyone is not willing to work, then he is not to eat, either."*

b) In I Timothy 5:3-13, Paul says needy elderly faithful widows should be supported, but not the young, those of poor repute, or those with family assets.

C. A Summary of the Old and New Testament Passages:

An Expositional Summary:

The Old Testament establishes a model for how God directed a nation to function in an orderly manner. To do so, God established ceremonial, moral and civil laws. We established in this chapter that the moral and civil laws are still relevant. In other words, the concepts shared in Exodus and Deuteronomy are still pertinant to the church today.

This is significant because God provides these principles to and for his people not to the unsaved. This is because the world is blind (II Corinthians 4:4) and God's thoughts are foolishness to them (II Corinthians 2:14). As a result it is imperative for God's people to dispense justice because God provided only to them his just Word (Amos 5:12-15; I Peter 4:17). When God's people do not dispense justice, God in the Old Testament states that he takes care of it himself (Jeremiah 5:28-29; Amos 8:4-6).

So each individual must function under the authority of God's Word as they relate to each other (each person has a moral responsible to their neighbor – Zechariah 7:9-10), and the church must remain focused on dispensing the will of God for the proper operation of God's people. It is when the people and the church accept God's plan that God empowers them to no longer experience oppression from their neighbors (Judges).

In the New Testament, Christ models for us his concern for those who were treated in an unjust manner as well as exposes his concern for the social needs of his people. In doing so, Christ does not follow the pattern that was consistently practiced during his stay on earth. As a result, Christ did not deserve judgment from God because he addressed injustice as God demanded each Jew to do in obedience to his moral and civil law. This model caused huge crowds to follow Christ because they became exposed to the true implementation of God's law.

Because the Church is a nation unto God (I Peter 2:9-10), and it establishes God's rule on earth. It is just as important for the church to address these issues as it was for the Old Testament Jews. It is when the church addresses these issues that the Gospel is more acceptable to the unsaved (I Peter 4:17), and the saints of God can truly operate as salt and light to the world (Matthew 5:13-16). If the church does not function under the authority of God's Word, then it becomes useless and good for nothing (Luke 14:34-35), and it is judged along with the world (I Corinthians 11:32). The church has a responsibility to be concerned about its own social issues (James 2:5-9; Galatians 2:1-14). It is when this is taken seriously that it truly functions as a pillar and foundation of truth (I Timothy 3:15) and practices true religion. *"If anyone thinks himself to be religious, and yet does not bridle his tongue but deceives his own heart, this man's religion is worthless. This is pure and undeflied religion in the sight of our God and Father, to visit orphans and widows in their distress, and to keep oneself unstained by the world"* (James 1:26-27).

When the church helps those in need (I John 3:16), feeds the hungry, clothes the naked (Matthew 25:31-46), addresses racism

(Galatians 2:11-14), partiality to the rich (James 2:5-9), cares for widows (I Timothy 5:1-9), helps the weak, confronts the unruly (I Thessalonians 5:14), judges its own issues (I Corinthians 6), takes care of those who are immoral (I Corinthians 5), helps those who are burdened (Galatians 6:2-4), empowers the rich share to with those who are in need (I Timothy 6:17-19), and addresses issues when the government violates individual's rights (Acts 21-28), the church is definitely positioned to address social issues and is also a powerful change agent. This is because the members of the church live in the same city as the church, go to jobs in the same city as the church and are expected to be salt and light. When these members are treated unfairly, they come to the only place that has a moral responsibility to help the weak, take care of the oppressed and to share their burden. When the church responds, it is no longer silent. When God's people are no longer silent evil does not prevail in the church or outside the church. *"Therefore, at such a time the prudent person keeps silent, for it is an evil time. Seek good and not evil, that you may live; and thus may the Lord God of host be with you, just as you have said"* (Amos 5:13).

General Summary:

We are not called to be God's policemen; vengence is his. Still, we are called to look out for our fellow man both believers and non-believers. We are to work for justice and plead the case of the "poor." This may be expanded to include the weak in general. We bear a particular responsibility to care for our brothers and sisters in Christ.

The primary focus should be on their well-being. The church may have a role to actively fight the perpetrators of injustice, but that role is secondary to caring for the victim. The church's responsibility is to the truly needy not the lazy or those with other assets.

III. A Practical Application for Church Policy Development

A. An individual who feels he/she is a victim of social injustice:

A complaint concerning the matter can be presented to a deacon, the assistant pastor, elder, associate pastor or the pastor. Once the complaint has been clearly outlined, a written document is established which formalizes the process before the elders.The matter needs to be brought to the pastor's attention who in turn will discuss the matter with the elders. The elder's ministry may handle the complaint themselves or refer it to a standing committee. The complaint will be evaluated regarding whether it is legitimate, and whether or not the victim is without resources to handle the matter.

B. When the complaint is legitimate:

1. When the complaint is legitimate, both the individual's resources and the church's resources will be considered.

2. If the victim has unutilized resources, he/she will be encouraged to use them before the church offers assistence. This includes such things as personal, family, business, and government financial or intellectual resources.

3. If the victim is without resources, the church will consider what resources it has available that may be used.

   a) The church may offer financial aid within the confines of good stewardship of the church's money. In most cases, this would include a minimum support to help the person through the effects of the injustice rather than money for a protracted legal battle or other fight against the offender. That is; the well being of the victim is the primary consideration.

   b) The church will involve its Social Service Ministry where ever needed.

   c) The church may offer non-financial resources through congregational volunteers. At or before a request for help the congregation might be polled regarding a willingness to offer their expertise on an as-needed basis. The church membership includes a wide range of professions, e.g., carpenters, accountants, movers, lawyers, and medical personnel.

C. Our hypothetical example may be revisted in light of the church policy.

The widow presented her complaint to the elder board. She was a godly long time member of the church with an excellent reputation for honesty and integrity. It was well known that her finances were limited and that she managed her meager funds carefully. She had no living children or other family support. The elder board checked its volunteer list and found an attorney. The attorney called the landlord but the landlord stood firm. The attorney felt a court victory was assured but would be too expensive for the church and not the best use of the church's money. Returning to the volunteer list, the elders found one volunteer to help the widow find a new apartment and others to help her move. The church also provided $600 dollars to help cover some of the moving expenses. The solution wasn't perfect, but was a good example of the church taking care of its own under difficult circumstances and with limited resources.

ABOUT THE AUTHOR

Dr. Paul Cannings is pastor of Living Word Fellowship Church in Houston, Texas. He is the president of Power Walk Ministries, a ministry for Church Leadership Development, Marriage and Family and Teacher's Training. He serves as a Bible Study Leader on KHCB - 105.7 FM 10:00 a.m., on Thursday mornings, The Pastor's Corner, Saturdays at 4:15 p.m. and he is the host of a live question and answer program – The Pastor's Study on Tuesday nights at 9:30 p.m., all in Houston, Texas. Dr. Cannings can also be heard on KTEK-1110 AM in Houston, Texas. He presently serves as Professor and Faculty Advisor at the College of Biblical Studies (formerly Houston Bible Institute).

He has served as youth director at Oak Cliff Bible Fellowship Church, Assistant Academic Dean of Dallas Bible College, Executive Vice President of Houston Bible Institute, National Director of Outreach ~ The Urban Alternative, and City Director for The Urban Alternative, Houston Branch. Cannings is the publisher of two series, "Leadership Training" for training leaders and "Keeping Love Alive" for strengthening marriages. Cannings and his wife Everette are the parents of two sons, Paul Jr., and Pierre. Cannings educational background includes:Oxford Graduate School, D. Phil.; Theological Studies in Religion & Society; Oxford University, England, Course Work Research; Dallas Theological Seminary, Th.M, Bible & Christian Education; Austin College, Bachelor of Arts.

www.ingramcontent.com/pod-product-compliance
Lightning Source LLC
Chambersburg PA
CBHW031252090426
42742CB00007B/420

* 9 7 8 0 9 7 7 9 8 4 0 3 9 *